すぐに使える
接客日本語会話
大特訓 英語版
決まり文句700

Conversational Customer Service Japanese Intensive Training
for Immediate Use [English Version]
700 Set Phrases

水谷信子 監修・著
Mizutani Nobuko

高橋尚子／スーザン・マスト／
Takahashi Naoko　Susan Mast

有田聡子／寺田則子 共著
Arita Satoko　Terada Noriko

Jリサーチ出版

はじめに
Foreword

　国際化の進んだ現在の日本では、多くの場面で外国から来た人々が活躍しているのを見ることができます。これまでは外国から来た人々が働くのは、工場などの生産の場やオフィスなどビジネスの場が主な場面だと思われていましたが、最近では次第にあらゆる産業・職種にわたって海外からの人の働く姿を見るようになりました。

　教育やレジャー、語学やスポーツ、趣味などを含めた広い意味でのサービス産業でも、今や多くの海外出身の人たちが大いに活躍しています。ただ、海外出身の人が日本人と同じ立場で仕事をするには、いうまでもなく、高度の日本語力がなくてはなりません。とくにサービス産業で働くとなれば、いっそうの会話力、コミュニケーション力が必要になります。こうした皆さんのために役に立つものをというわたしたちの願いが実を結んだのがこの小さな冊子です。

　小さい冊子の限られた紙面ですが、考えられる限りのさまざまな接客場面を具体的に取り上げ、実際の会話を再現し、とくに役に立つ表現を集めて紹介するようにしました。これらの表現を身に付けて職場で活用してくだされば、必ずや客の満足を得ることができます。皆さんが日本のサービス産業の職場で生き生きと働く姿を想像して、わたしたちは心ときめく思いでこの冊子をお届けします。ご成功を信じています。

水谷信子

Now that Japan has become a more international country, one can now see individuals from other countries working in many scenarios. While it was once thought that those from abroad came to work at factories in industrial jobs or at offices in business jobs, it is now common to see such people working in a large variety of industries and jobs.

Many individuals coming from overseas are now active even in the service industry, broadly defined as encompassing education, leisure, language, sports, hobbies, and more. However, it goes without saying that in order for such individuals to work in the same positions as Japanese people, they must be able to use the Japanese language at a high level. In particular, working in the service industry requires an even higher level of conversation and communication abilities. This small publication came out of our hope to be of use to those who are in this position such as you, the reader.

While there are only so many pages in this small publication, we highlight every varied customer service situation that we could think of, reproducing actual conversations and introducing a collection of expressions that could be particularly useful. By learning these expressions for yourself and using them in the workplace, we are sure that you will be able to satisfy your customers. We bring you this publication with excitement in our hearts as we think of its readers energetically working in the Japanese service industry, and we hope for your success.

Nobuko Mizutani

目次
Contents

本書の使い方 ・・・・・・・・・・・・ 8
How to Use This Book

序章　日本的接客サービスの心がまえ ・・・・・・・ 10
The Attitude Behind Japanese Customer Service

第1章　敬語の基本パターンと接客の基本表現 ・・・・ 15
Basic Respectful Language Patterns and Basic Customer Service Expressions

Unit 1 敬語① ・・・・・・・・・・・ 16
Honorific Language 1: the form of "o- + V-~~masu~~ + kudasai" and "go- + V-~~suru~~ + kudasai"

Unit 2 敬語② ・・・・・・・・・・・ 18
Honorific Language 2: the form of "o- + V-~~masu~~ + ni naru" and "go- + V-~~suru~~ + ni naru"

Unit 3 敬語③ ・・・・・・・・・・・ 20
Honorific Language 3: Special expressions

Unit 4 敬語④ ・・・・・・・・・・・ 22
Honorific Language 4: "-reru/-rareru" form and "~~nasaru/sareru~~" form

Unit 5 敬語⑤ ・・・・・・・・・・・ 24
Honorific Language 5: Humble expressons

Unit 6 敬語⑥ ・・・・・・・・・・・ 26
Honorific Language 6: Polite Expressions

Unit 7 客を迎える・客を見送る ・・・ 28
Greeting Customers / Seeing Customers Off

Unit 8 営業時間 ・・・・・・・・・・ 30
Operating Hours

Unit 9 トイレの案内 ・・・・・・・・ 32
Guiding Customers to the Restroom

Unit 10 よく聞き取れない・わからない ・・・・・・・・ 34
When Something is Hard to Hear / When You Can't Understand

Unit 11 よく使うひとこと表現① ・・ 36
Frequently Used Short Expressions 1

Unit 12 よく使うひとこと表現② ・・ 38
Frequently Used Short Expressions 2

Unit 13 会計① ・・・・・・・・・・ 40
Checking Out 1: Using a Card

Unit 14 会計② ・・・・・・・・・・ 42
Checking Out 2: Using Cash

Unit 15 会計③ ・・・・・・・・・・ 44
Checking Out 3: Other

Unit 16 謝る ・・・・・・・・・・・ 46
Apologizing

第2章　飲食店 ・・・・・・・・ 49
Restaurant

Unit 1 飲食店の基本① ・・・・・・・ 50
Restaurant Basics 1: Handling Phone Reservations

Unit 2 飲食店の基本② ・・・・・・・ 52
Restaurant Basics 2: Guiding Visitors 1

Unit 3 飲食店の基本③ ・・・・・・・ 54
Restaurant Basics 3: Guiding Visitors 2

Unit 4	飲食店の基本④ ・・・・・・ 56
	Restaurant Basics 4: When a Restaurant is Full
Unit 5	飲食店の基本⑤ ・・・・・・ 58
	Restaurant Basics 5: Taking Orders 1
Unit 6	飲食店の基本⑥ ・・・・・・ 60
	Restaurant Basics 6: Taking Orders 2
Unit 7	飲食店の基本⑦ ・・・・・・ 62
	Restaurant Basics 7: Taking Orders 3
Unit 8	飲食店の基本⑧ ・・・・・・ 64
	Restaurant Basics 8: Bringing Dishes
Unit 9	飲食店の基本⑨ ・・・・・・ 66
	Restaurant Basics 9: Small Acts of Service
Unit 10	飲食店の基本⑩ ・・・・・・ 68
	Restaurant Basics 10: Making Customers Wait Briefly
Unit 11	飲食店の基本⑪ ・・・・・・ 70
	Restaurant Basics 11: Changing Orders
Unit 12	飲食店の基本⑫ ・・・・・・ 72
	Restaurant Basics 12: Dealing with Complaints
Unit 13	飲食店の基本⑬ ・・・・・・ 74
	Restaurant Basics 13: Dealing with Complaints
Unit 14	飲食店の基本⑭ ・・・・・・ 76
	Restaurant Basics 14: Other
Unit 15	ファーストフード店① ・・・・ 78
	Fast Food Stores 1: Hamburger Shops, Etc. 1
Unit 16	ファーストフード店② ・・・・ 80
	Fast Food Stores 2: Hamburger Shops, Etc.
Unit 17	ファーストフード店③ ・・・・ 82
	Fast Food Stores 3: Udon, Soba, Beef Bowls, etc.
Unit 18	居酒屋① ・・・・・・・・・・ 84
	Izakaya 1: Ordering Alcohol 1
Unit 19	居酒屋② ・・・・・・・・・・ 86
	Izakaya 2: Ordering Alcohol 2
Unit 20	居酒屋③ ・・・・・・・・・・ 88
	Izakaya 3: Food Orders and Explaining Food 1
Unit 21	居酒屋④ ・・・・・・・・・・ 90
	Izakaya 4: Food Orders and Explaining Food 2
Unit 22	居酒屋⑤ ・・・・・・・・・・ 92
	Izakaya 5: Other
Unit 23	パブ ・・・・・・・・・・・・ 94
	Pubs: Ordering Drinks

単語＆ミニフレーズ・・・・・・・・ 96
Vocabulary + Mini-Phrases

第3章 販売店
Store

Unit 1	販売店の基本① ・・・・・・・ 100
	Store Basics 1: Simple Phrases Used on Store Floors
Unit 2	販売店の基本② ・・・・・・・ 102
	Store Basics 2: Products and Services
Unit 3	販売店の基本③ ・・・・・・・ 104
	Store Basics 3: Stock
Unit 4	販売店の基本④ ・・・・・・・ 106
	Store Basics 4: Product Packaging
Unit 5	販売店の基本⑤ ・・・・・・・ 108
	Store Basics 5: Product Shipping
Unit 6	販売店の基本⑥ ・・・・・・・ 110
	Store Basics 6: Other, Service at the Register
Unit 7	販売店の基本⑦ ・・・・・・・ 112
	Store Basics 7: Dealing with Demands for Returns or Lower Prices

Unit 8 アパレル① ･････････ 114
Apparel 1: Suggesting Products

Unit 9 アパレル② ･････････ 116
Apparel 2: Materials

Unit 10 アパレル③ ･････････ 118
Apparel 3: Trying Clothes On

Unit 11 アパレル④ ･････････ 120
Apparel 4: Color / Design

Unit 12 アパレル⑤ ･････････ 122
Apparel 5: Shoes

Unit 13 アパレル⑥ ･････････ 124
Apparel 6: Bags

Unit 14 雑貨店 ･･･････････ 126
General Stores

Unit 15 ドラッグストア① ･･････ 128
Drugstores 1: Symptoms

Unit 16 ドラッグストア② ･･････ 130
Drugstores 2: Questions about Medicine

Unit 17 ドラッグストア③ ･･････ 132
Drugstores 3: Explaining Medicine

Unit 18 ドラッグストア④ ･･････ 134
Drugstores 4: Other

Unit 19 化粧品店 ･･･････････ 136
Cosmetics Shop

Unit 20 スーパー① ･･･････････ 138
Supermarkets 1

Unit 21 スーパー② ･･･････････ 140
Supermarkets 2

Unit 22 スーパー③ ･･･････････ 142
Supermarkets 3

Unit 23 家電量販店① ･･････ 144
Consumer Electronics Retailer 1

Unit 24 家電量販店② ･･････ 146
Consumer Electronics Retailer 2

単語＆ミニフレーズ ･････････ 148
Vocabulary + Mini-Phrases

第4章 コンビニ ･････････ 151
Convenience Stores

Unit 1 コンビニ① ･･････････ 152
Convenience Stores 1: Registers 1

Unit 2 コンビニ② ･･････････ 154
Convenience Stores 2: Registers 2

Unit 3 コンビニ③ ･･････････ 156
Convenience Stores 3: Registers 3

Unit 4 コンビニ④ ･･････････ 158
Convenience Stores 4: Food and Drink

Unit 5 コンビニ⑤ ･･････････ 160
Convenience Stores 5: Deliveries and Copies

単語＆ミニフレーズ ･････････ 162
Vocabulary + Mini-Phrases

第5章 宿泊施設 ･････････ 163
Accommodations

Unit 1 宿泊施設① ･･････････ 164
Accommodations 1: Taking Reservations on the Phone 1

Unit 2 宿泊施設② ･･････････ 166
Accommodations 2: Taking Reservations on the Phone 2

Unit 3 宿泊施設③ ･･････････ 168
Accommodations 3: Checking in

Unit 4 宿泊施設④ ･･････････ 170
Accommodations 4: SOS from Rooms

Unit 5 宿泊施設⑤ ･･････････ 172
Accommodations 5: Requests from Rooms

Unit 6 宿泊施設⑥ ・・・・・・・・ 174
Accommodations 6: Other

単語＆ミニフレーズ・・・・・・・・ 176
Vocabulary + Mini-Phrases

第6章 その他のさまざまなサービス ・・・・・・・・ 177
Various Other Services

Unit 1 カラオケ店① ・・・・・・・・ 178
Karaoke Stores 1: Reception

Unit 2 カラオケ店② ・・・・・・・・ 180
Karaoke 2: Explaining How to Use the Facilities

Unit 3 レンタルビデオ店① ・・・・・ 182
Rental Video Store 1: Handling Customers on the Sales Floor / Card Procedures

Unit 4 レンタルビデオ店② ・・・・・ 184
Rental Video Store 2: Confirming Use and Checkout

Unit 5 講座① ・・・・・・・・・・ 186
Instructors 1: Language Instruction

Unit 6 講座② ・・・・・・・・・・ 188
Instructors 2: Various Instruction

Unit 7 講座③ ・・・・・・・・・・ 190
Instructors 3: Various Instruction

単語＆ミニフレーズ・・・・・・・・ 192
Vocabulary + Mini-Phrases

第7章 電話基本会話 ・・・・・・ 193
Basic Telephone Conversations

Unit 1 電話応対① ・・・・・・・・ 194
Answering the Phone 1: Taking Reservations at a Restaurant

Unit 2 電話応対② ・・・・・・・・ 196
Answering the Phone 2: Taking Reservations at a Hotel

Unit 3 電話応対③ ・・・・・・・・ 198
Answering the Phone 3: When Someone is Not Present

Unit 4 電話応対④ ・・・・・・・・ 200
Answering the Phone 4: Messages

Unit 5 電話応対⑤ ・・・・・・・・ 202
Answering the Phone 5: Other

単語＆ミニフレーズ・・・・・・・・ 204
Vocabulary + Mini-Phrases

第8章 緊急・トラブル ・・・・ 205
Emergencies / Trouble

Unit 1 急病人① ・・・・・・・・・ 206
Emergency Cases 1: Speaking to Individuals

Unit 2 急病人② ・・・・・・・・・ 208
Emergency Cases 2: Confirmation

Unit 3 地震 ・・・・・・・・・・・ 210
Earthquakes: Basic Responses When an Earthquake Strikes

Unit 4 火災 ・・・・・・・・・・・ 212
Fires: Basic Responses Regarding Fires

Unit 5 避難 ・・・・・・・・・・・ 214
Evacuating: Evacuating Safely

Unit 6 落とし物・忘れ物 ・・・・・ 216
Lost and Forgotten Items

単語＆ミニフレーズ・・・・・・・・ 218
Vocabulary + Mini-Phrases

丁寧表現早見表 ・・・・・・・・・ 219
Polite Language Reference Sheet

本書の使い方
How to Use This Book

本書ではまず、第1章「敬語の基本パターンと接客の基本表現」で接客日本語会話の基礎固めをします。その後の第2章から第8章までは、業種や職業などをもとに実際的な接客場面を再現しながら、フレーズの練習をしていきます。

This book begins by teaching the fundamentals of conversational customer service Japanese in Chapter 1: "Basic Patterns of Polite Speech and Basic Customer Service Expressions." Next, Chapters 2 through 8 recreate realistic customer service situations based on individual industries and jobs so that you can practice specific phrases.

① 英語表現／English Expression

右ページの日本語フレーズの英訳です。なるべく自然な英語表現にしています。

The page on the right has English translations of the Japanese phrases. These expressions are in natural English.

② 日本語表現のヒント／Tips for Japanese Expressions

フレーズの中でポイントになる語を取り上げ、「英語→日本語」の形で示しています。

Important tips within individual phrases are highlighted and indicated in an English to Japanese format.

③ 頭出しのヒント／Initial Phrase Tips

日本語フレーズの頭の部分を示しています。くり返し練習をする中で、だんだん見ないで言えるようにしましょう。

The initial parts of Japanese phrases are indicated. Practice these so that you learn to say them without having to look at them.

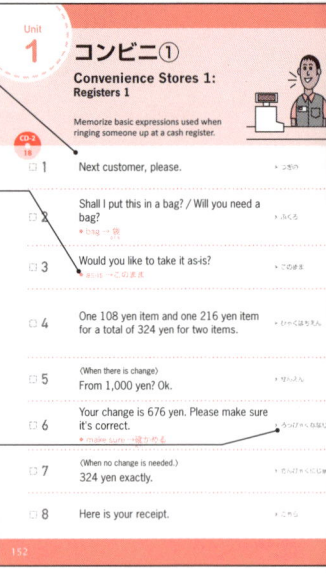

付属の CD / Attached CD

音声は「英語→日本語」の順で流れます。英語の後、少しポーズがありますので、自分で日本語で言ってみましょう。それから、日本語の音声で確認します。

The voice on the CD first speaks in English, then in Japanese. There is a short pause after the English, so take this opportunity to say the phrase in Japanese before then confirming it based on the voice on the CD.

英語／English	⇒	ポーズ／Pause	⇒	日本語／Japanese
言いたいことをイメージする〈やや速め〉 **Visualize what you want to say** 〈Slightly fast〉		この間に言う **Say it here**		確認する〈落ち着いた、丁寧な話し方〉 **Confirm** 〈A calm and polite way of speaking〉

★ 音声ダウンロードの案内は、本の一番後ろの部分にあります。

Information on how to download voice information can be found in the back of this book.

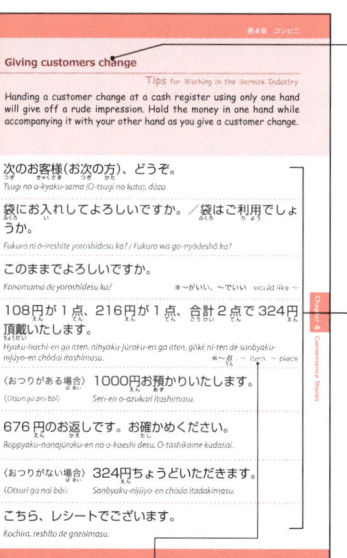

④ 接客ワンポイントアドバイス／Thips for Working in the Service Industry

場面や日本語フレーズに関連する接客サービスのポイントを紹介します。

Advice regarding customer service situations and Japanese phrases is introduced here.

⑤ 日本語フレーズ／Japanese Phrases

場面や機能などで分類された 92 のユニットで紹介します。全部で約 700 フレーズあります。

92 units are introduced here separated by situation, function, and so on. There are a total of about 700 phrases.

⑥ 日本語キーワード／Japanese Keywords

やや難しいものや注意を要するものを取り上げ、個別に対訳を付けています。

Terms that are somewhat difficult or that require special attention are highlighted here and individually translated.

日本式接客サービスの心がまえ
The Attitude Behind Japanese Customer Service

　日本で接客の仕事をするには、言うまでもなく、お客様に接することについて日本人がどう考えているか、どう感じているかをよく知っておくことが大切です。「おもてなし」ということばに表れている日本人の考え方と、そこから生まれる言葉遣いや態度などについて、よく理解しておくことが接客の仕事の成功に通じます。

1．おもてなしの心

　お客様と店員の関係は通常、お金を払ってサービスを受ける「顧客」とサービスを提供する「接客業者」という、いわばビジネスの関係だということができます。しかしお客様に対する日本人の気持ちには、お客を単なるビジネスの相手とみなすのでなく、家庭を訪問してくれたお客様を迎えるようにすべきだという考えがあります。「訪問者を大切にする」という「おもてなし」は、そこから来ています。わざわざ訪問してくれたお客様に対しては、ただビジネスとしてのサービスを提供するのでなく、できるだけ快適に過ごしてもらえるよう努力すべきだという考えの表れです。

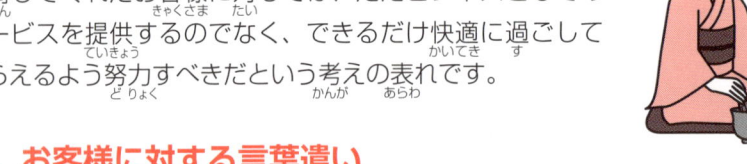

2．お客様に対する言葉遣い

　お客様に対する店員の言葉遣いは、丁寧でなければなりません。お客様に対する特に丁寧な言葉遣いを身につけるのは、店員にとって大変面倒なことですが、非常に大切なことです。詳しくは本の中で紹介しますが、一例として次のような特別の言葉遣いができるようになるのが、接客の仕事の第一歩だということができます。

❶ 文の形

　文の形も特別なものを使います。ふつうの話では、文の終わりには「です」や「ます」を使い、たとえば

　　「店内は禁煙です」
　　「当店は 10 時に閉店します」

のような言い方をしますが、これでは特別に相手を大切にする気持ちが表れませんので、お客様に対してはもっと丁寧な表現を使い、

　　「店内は禁煙でございます」　「当店は 10 時に閉店いたします」

のように改まった言い方をします。

❷ 相手に関すること

　相手はお客様ですから、人数について言うときは

　　「何人」でなく「何名様」
　　「ひとり」でなく「おひとり様」

のように言います。また、お客様に関する言葉として

　　「子ども」でなく「お子様」
　　「連れ」でなく「お連れ様」

のように、「様」を付けて敬意を表す表現を使います。
　また、お客様の持ち物などについても

　　「お荷物」「おかばん」

のように「お」を付けたり、お客様の気持ちについても

　　「ご希望」「ご満足」

のように「ご」を付けるなど、丁寧な言葉遣いが必要です。
　詳しいことは各場面の例文で勉強してもらいますが、こうした特別な言葉遣いは、決してお客様を「よそもの」として遠ざけるものではなく、お客様を大切にする態度の表れですから、心をこめて使うようにしてください。

３．お客様に対する態度

　お客様に対しては、買い物や食事などの時間を気持ちよく過ごしてもらえるよう、店員は最大の努力をしなければなりません。態度として特に気をつける点は、次のようなことです。

　　「なるべく気に入った品物や料理を選んでいただく」
　　「最上の品物や料理に満足感を持っていただく」
　　「できるだけ待たせたり、我慢させたりしない」
　　「待つ、などの不便をお願いするときは丁寧にお願いする」

のようなことです。どの場合も皆さんが、自分がお客の立場に立ったらどう感じるかということを常に考えるようにすれば、こうした心遣いはおおげさでなく、当然のことと感じられるでしょう。

４．感じのよい接し方

　接客の職場で働く皆さんが、感じのよい態度でお客様を迎えることができるように、また、お客様によい店員だと思ってもらえるように、という願いから、以下の練習や説明を用意しました。これを生かして、「おもてなしの心」のある感じのよい接し方を身につけるようにしてください。その結果、「お客様」が喜んでくれれば、皆さんの働く職場が明るくなるでしょう。

　It goes without saying that when working in customer service in Japan, it is important to have a close understanding of how Japanese people think and feel as you deal with them as customers. Understanding Japanese peoples' thoughts regarding the term omotenashi (hospitality) and the way of speaking and acting that comes from these thoughts will play a direct role in your success in customer service jobs.

1. A Heart of Hospitality

The relationship between a customer and an employee can normally be seen as a businesslike one between a consumer, who pays money to receive services, and a service provider, who offers those services. However, Japanese people do not see customers as simple partners in a business exchange, and instead think that they should be received as one might receive a visitor to their own home. This is where the idea of hospitality, valuing those who come to visit you, comes from. It is an expression of the idea that because a customer made the choice to visit your establishment, you should work to make their experience as pleasant as possible, instead of simply providing them with services as a business.

2. Language Used With Customers

Store employees must use polite language to customers. It may be very difficult for an employee to learn the particularly polite language used to customers, but it is very important to do so. More detail will be given later in this book, but the first step toward a job in customer service is the kind of unique language usage demonstrated below.

❶ Sentence Form

A unique sentence form is used when speaking to customers. In normal speech, sentences end with desu and masu, such as

「店内は禁煙でございます」(This store is non-smoking)
「当店は10時に閉店いたします」(This store closes at 10)

However, these do not indicate any feelings of valuing one's customers in a special way, so more polite expressions are used when speaking to customers, such as

「店内は禁煙でございます」(This store is non-smoking)
「当店は10時に閉店いたします」(This store closes at 10)

❷ Words Relating to Others

Because you are speaking to a customer, when referring to a number of people, use

「何名様」instead of「何人」(How many people)
「おひとり様」instead of「ひとり」(One person)

Also, when referring to customers, use

「お子様(こさま)」 instead of 「子(こ)ども」 (Child)
「お連(つ)れ様(さま)」 instead of 「連(つ)れ」 (Companion)

As seen above, add 「様(さま)」 to indicate your respect for your customers.

Also, when referring to a customer's belongings, add 「お」 such as

「お荷物(にもつ)」「おかばん」 (Luggage) (Bag)

Also add 「ご」 when referring to a customer's feelings, such as

「ご希望(きぼう)」「ご満足(まんぞく)」 (Desire / Satisfaction)

Doing so will make your words more polite.

While you will learn this in more detail through example sentences for various scenarios, this unique way of speaking is meant to show an attitude of valuing customers instead of seeing them as distant "outsiders," so use these phrases wholeheartedly.

3. Attitude Toward Customers

Store employees must do their best to make sure customers can enjoy their time shopping, eating, and so on. An employee must be particularly careful about things such as the following when it comes to their attitude.

- Have customers select items or dishes they are as interested as possible in.
- Satisfy customers with the best items and dishes.
- Keep customers from having to wait or endure as much as possible.
- When asking customers for something that will inconvenience them, such as asking them to wait, do it in a polite way.

If you always keep in mind how you would feel if you were in the customer's shoes, it should be easy to feel how this kind of consideration is a natural thing, and not something exaggerated.

4. Pleasant Contact

We have prepared the following practice exercises and explanations out of our hope that readers such as you will learn how to receive customers with a good attitude and how to be thought of as a good employee by customers. Please make use of these to interact with your customers in a pleasant, hospitable way. If you can do so and delight your customers as a result, we are sure that your workplace will become
a brighter one.

第1章

敬語の基本パターンと接客の基本表現

Basic Respectful Language Patterns and Basic Customer Service Expressions

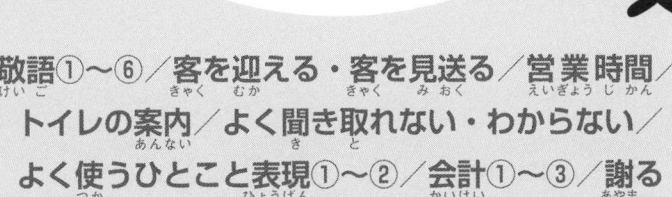

敬語①〜⑥／客を迎える・客を見送る／営業時間／
トイレの案内／よく聞き取れない・わからない／
よく使うひとこと表現①〜②／会計①〜③／謝る

Honorific Language 1-6 / Greeting Customers /
Operating Hours / Guiding Customers to the Restroom /
When Something is Hard to Hear / When You Can't Understand /
Frequently Used Short Expressions 1-2 /
Checking Out 1-3 / Apologizing

Unit 1

敬語①
けいご

Honorific Language 1:
the form of "*o-* + V-~~masu~~ + *kudasai*"
and "*go-* + V-~~suru~~ + *kudasai*"

This keigo pattern indicates actions by the person who is being addressed.

CD-1 / 2

☐ 1 Please wait a moment. ▸ しょうしょう

☐ 2 Please take this number. ▸ こちらの

☐ 3 Please have a seat here. ▸ こちらに
● have a seat（→すわる）→かける

☐ 4 Please select one of these. ▸ このなか

☐ 5 Please take this opportunity. ▸ ぜひ
● opportunity →機会
　　　　　　　きかい

☐ 6 Please check whether it is correct. ▸ まちがい

☐ 7 Please understand that sales will end as soon as the inventory is sold out. ▸ ざいこ
● as soon as 〜→〜次第、〜（する）とすぐに
　　　　　　　　しだい

☐ 8 Please contact us as soon as possible if there are any changes or cancellations. ▸ へんこう
● cancellation →キャンセル

"O~kudasai" "go~kudasai"

Tips for Working in the Service Industry

"O~kudasai" "go~kudasai" are used very often in customer service situations. A simple way to remember them is to use "go~kudasai" for "~suru" verbs, and to use "o~kudasai" for other verbs.

少々お待ちください。
Shōshō o-machi kudasai.

こちらの番号札をお持ちください。
Kochira no bangōfuda o o-mochi kudasai.

＊番号札：number ticket

こちらにおかけください。
Kochira ni o-kake kudasai.

この中から一つお選びください。
Kono naka kara hitotsu o-erabi kudasai.

ぜひ、この機会をご利用ください。
Zehi, kono kikai o go-riyō kudasai.

間違いがないか、ご確認ください。
Machigai ga naika, go-kakunin kudasai.

在庫がなくなり次第、販売終了となります。ご了承ください。
Zaiko ga nakunari shidai, hanbai shūryō to narimasu. Go-ryōshō kudasai.

変更やキャンセルの場合は、早めにご連絡ください。
Henkō ya kyanseru no bāi wa, hayameni go-renraku kudasai.

＊変更：alteration, change

Unit 2

敬語②
けいご

Honorific Language 2:
the form of "o- + V-masu + ni naru" and "go- + V-suru + ni naru"

This keigo pattern indicates actions or intentions on the part of the person who is being addressed.

CD-1 / 3

☐ **1** Would you like to wait? ▸ おまち…

☐ **2** Do you want to quit/stop? ▸ おやめ…

☐ **3** Will you pay in cash?
  • in cash → 現金で
  げんきん
  ▸ げんきん

☐ **4** Would you like to try a different size?
  • try → 試す
  ため
  ▸ べつの

☐ **5** Would you like to use one of our grocery bags? ▸ レジぶくろ

☐ **6** Did you make a mistake? Then please write it again here. ▸ おまちがえ

☐ **7** Will you be using chopsticks? ▸ おはし

☐ **8** Would you like to see a menu? ▸ メニュー

"O~ni narimasu" "go~ni narimasu"

Tips for Working in the Service Industry

"O~ni narimasu" "go~ni narimasu" are one form of respectful language and avoid directly referring to someone's actions or deeds.

お待ちになりますか。
O-machi ni narimasu ka?

おやめになりますか。
O-yame ni narimasu ka?

現金でお支払いになりますか。
Genkin de o-shiharai ni narimasu ka?

別のサイズをお試しになりますか。
Betsu no saizu o o-tameshi ni narimasu ka?

＊別の：different

レジ袋はお使いになりますか。
Reji-bukuro wa o-tsukai ni narimasu ka?

お間違えになりましたか。では、こちらにもう一度お書きください。
O-machigae ni narimashita ka? Dewa, kochira ni mō ichido o-kaki kudasai.

お箸はご利用になりますか。
O-hashi wa go-riyō ni narimasu ka?

メニューをご覧になりますか。
Menyū o go-ran ni narimasu ka?

Unit 3

敬語③
けいご
Honorific Language:
Special expressions

In keigo, even some ordinary words are replaced with special expressions.

☐ 1 About what time will you be at home?
 • About what time ...? → 何時ごろ（なら）…か
   なんじ
▸ なんじごろ

☐ 2 Is this your first time here?
▸ こちらに

☐ 3 Would you like to eat dessert?
▸ デザート

☐ 4 I'm sorry, what did you say?
▸ すみません

☐ 5 What sort of clothing does your mother generally wear?
 • What sort of clothing ...? → どんな服…か
   ふく
▸ おかあさま

☐ 6 Please have a look if you have time.
▸ おじかん

☐ 7 Are you aware that this kind of service is available?
▸ こういう

☐ 8 Thank you for coming such a long way.
▸ とおくから

20

Memorize special words as-is

Tips for Working in the Service Industry

Some verbs are not used at all in *keigo*, but instead are replaced with completely different words. These are used frequently in daily conversation, so try to remember them one at a time.

何時ごろなら、ご自宅にいらっしゃいますか。
Nan-ji goro nara, go-jitaku ni irasshaimasu ka?   ＊いらっしゃる：いる

こちらにいらっしゃったのは初めてですか。
Kochira ni irasshatta no wa hajimete desu ka?   ＊いらっしゃる：来る

デザートはお召し上がりになりますか。
Dezāto wa o-meshiagari ni narimasu ka?   ＊召し上がる：食べる

すみません、何とおっしゃいましたか。
Sumimasen, nan to osshaimashita ka?

お母様はいつもどんな服をお召しになっていますか。
O-kāsama wa itsumo donna fuku o o-meshi ni natte imasu ka?   ＊お召しになる：着る

お時間があれば、ぜひご覧ください。
O-jikan ga areba, zehi go-ran kudasai.

こういうサービスがあるのはご存じでしょうか。
Kōiu sābisu ga aru no wa go-zonji deshō ka?

遠くからお越しいただき、ありがとうございます。
Tōku kara o-koshi itadaki, arigatō gozaimasu.

Unit 4

敬語 ④
けいご

Honorific Language 4:
"*-reru/-rareru*" form and "*nasaru/sareru*" form

The verb endings *-reru/-rareru* and the forms *nasaru/sareru* replacing *suru* are also used in keigo.

CD-1 5

☐ 1　Everyone is surprised that there is so much.　▶ りょう

☐ 2　Have you already visited this art museum?　▶ こちらの

☐ 3　Many people are here for the first time.　▶ はじめて

☐ 4　It seems that the others have already gone home.　▶ ほかの
　　　● a little while ago → 先ほど、少し前に
　　　　　　　　　　　　　　さき　　すこ まえ

☐ 5　What will you do? / What will you choose?　▶ いかが

☐ 6　What would you like to drink?　▶ おのみもの

☐ 7　Have you already registered?　▶ とうろく

☐ 8　Will you cancel?　▶ キャンセル

"*reru*" "*rareru*" and "*nasaru*" "*sareru*"

Tips for Working in the Service Industry

"*Ikareru/*行かれる" and "*korareru/*来られる" can also be said as "*irassharu.*" This also applies to "*nasaru*" and "*sareru*". There is no need to be nervous about distinguishing between them.

量が多いので、皆さん、驚か**れ**ます。
Ryō ga ōi node, minasan, odorokaremasu.

こちらの美術館にはもう行か**れ**ましたか。
Kochira no bijutsukan ni wa mō ikaremashita ka?

初めて来**られ**たという方が多いです。
Hajimete korareta toiu kata ga ōi desu.

ほかの方々は先ほど帰**られ**たようです。
Hoka no katagata wa sakihodo kaerareta yō desu.

いかが**なさいます**か。
Ikaga nasaimasu ka?

お飲み物は何に**なさいます**か。
O-nomimono wa nani ni nasaimasu ka?

登録はもう**されました**か。
Tōroku wa mō saremashita ka?

＊登録（する）: to register

キャンセル**されます**か。
Kyanseru saremasu ka?

Unit 5

敬語⑤
けいご

Honorific Language:
Humble expressons

These are the basic forms of humble speech, which indicates respect for the person being addressed through humility for one's own actions and attitudes.

CD-1 6

☐ **1** We are grateful to receive your reservation. ▶ ごよやく

☐ **2** 〈On the phone〉
I will read the number. Are you ready to write it down?
- Are you ready? → 用意はいいですか。
- to write down → メモ(する)

▶ ばんごう

☐ **3** I look forward to your next visit to our shop. ▶ またの

☐ **4** 〈About a place〉
I will show you where it is.

▶ ごあんない…

☐ **5** May I ask your name? ▶ おなまえ

☐ **6** We are handing out discount coupons today.
- hand out（→くばる）→さしあげる

▶ ほんじつ

☐ **7** May I see your card? ▶ カード

☐ **8** I will go there now. Please wait a moment. ▶ ただいま

Humble language

Tips for Working in the Service Industry

Humble language places yourself in a lower position in order to show respect for those you are talking to. Use it when talking about your own actions or about yourself.

ご予約をいただき、ありがとうございます。
Go-yoyaku o itadaki, arigatō gozaimasu.

〈電話で〉番号を申し上げます。メモのご用意はよろしいでしょうか。
〈*denwa de*〉 *Bangō o mōshiagemasu. Memo no go-yōi wa yoroshī deshō ka?*

またのご来店をお待ちしております。
Mata no go-raiten o o-machi shite orimasu.

〈場所について〉ご案内します。
〈*Basho ni tsuite*〉 *Go-annai shimasu.*

お名前をお伺いしてもよろしいでしょうか。
O-namae o o-ukagai shitemo yoroshī deshō ka?

本日、割引券を差し上げております。
Honjitsu, waribikiken o sashiagete orimasu.

＊割引券：discount coupon, discount ticket

カードを拝見します。
Kādo o haiken shimasu.

ただ今参りますので、少々お待ちください。
Tadaima mairimasu node, shōshō o-machi kudasai.

Unit 6

敬語⑥
けいご

Honorific Language 6:
Polite Expressions

Polite expressions are used in customer service whenever anything is being said.

☐ 1　The restroom can be found down here.　▶ トイレ

☐ 2　That will be 3,500 yen with tax.　▶ ぜいこみ
　　　● with tax →税込で
　　　　　　　　　ぜいこみ

☐ 3　Thank you very much for today.　▶ ほんじつは
　　　● for today（→今日は）→本日は
　　　　　　　　　　きょう　　ほんじつ

☐ 4　This is an M size.　▶ こちらが

☐ 5　This is the drink menu.　▶ こちら

☐ 6　Would both of you like coffee?　▶ おふたかた
　　　● both of you（→お二人とも）→お二方とも
　　　　　　　　　　　　ふたり　　　　　ふたかた

☐ 7　Can I get you anything else? / Will that be everything?　▶ ごちゅうもん

☐ 8　I am unsure.　▶ わたくし

26

Polite language

Tips for Working in the Service Industry

Polite language is used when showing respect to someone you are speaking to or to be polite by using formal language. In polite language, you may use "*o*" or "*go*" before nouns and adjectives, as well as terms such as "*desu*", "*masu*", and "*gozaimasu*." However, "*o*" and "*go*" are not used with katakana words.

トイレは、この奥にございます。
Toire wa, kono oku ni gozaimasu.
　　＊ございます：the polite expression of "あります"　　＊この奥：the back of here

税込で 3500 円でございます。
Zēkomi de sanzen-gohyaku-en de gozaimasu.
　　　　　　　　　　＊〜でございます：the polite expression of "〜です"

本日は誠に ありがとうございます。
Honjitsu wa makotoni arigatō gozaimasu.

こちらが M サイズでございます。
Kochira ga emu saizu de gozaimasu.

こちら、お飲み物のメニューでございます。
Kochira, o-nomimono no menyū de gozaimasu.

お二方とも、コーヒーでよろしいでしょうか。
O-futakata tomo, kōhī de yoroshī deshō ka?

ご注文の品はお揃いでしょうか。
Go-chūmon no shina wa o-soroi deshō ka?

わたくしではわかりかねます。
Watakushi dewa wakari kanemasu.
　　　　＊〜かねます：Takes the form "〜ます(V)＋かねます."
　　　　　　　　　　Indicates feelings of not being able to do 〜.

Unit 7

客を迎える・客を見送る
きゃく　むか　　きゃく　み　おく

Greeting Customers / Seeing Customers Off

Memorize expressions to use when customers arrive and leave, since this helps to make a good impression.

CD-1 / 8

☐ 1　Welcome.　▶ いらっしゃい…

☐ 2　Please take your time.　▶ ごゆっくり

☐ 3　Please take your time and enjoy.　▶ ごゆっくり

☐ 4　If you need anything, please let me know.　▶ なにか
　　　• if you need anything →何かありましたら
　　　　　　　　　　　　　　　なに

☐ 5　Please make sure you aren't forgetting anything.　▶ おわすれもの

☐ 6　Thank you for coming to our store.　▶ ごらいてん

☐ 7　Thank you very much. Please come again.　▶ ありがとう…

☐ 8　Please be careful going home.　▶ おきをつけて

"Irasshaimase"

Tips for Working in the Service Industry

"*Irasshaimase*" is primarily used when 1: A customer enters a store 2: You begin speaking directly to a customer 3: When a customer begins to approach you (When either you pass by a customer or vice versa).

いらっしゃいませ。
Irasshaimase.

ごゆっくりどうぞ。
Go-yukkuri dōzo.

ごゆっくりお楽しみください。
Go-yukkuri o-tanoshimi kudasai.

何かありましたら、お申し付けください。
Nanika arimashitara, o-mōshitsuke kudasai.

＊申し付ける：Used to express when someone in a superior position gives a command or request to someone in a lower position.

お忘れ物はございませんか。
O-wasuremono wa gozaimasen ka?

ご来店ありがとうございました。
Go-raiten arigatō gozaimashita.

＊ご来店：the polite expression of "coming to the store"

ありがとうございました。またお越しくださいませ。
Arigatō gozaimashita. Mata o-koshi kudasaimase.

お気をつけてお帰りください。
O-ki o tsukete o-kaeri kudasai.

Unit 8

営業時間
えいぎょうじかん
Operating Hours

Memorize basic expressions to reply to frequently-asked questions about operating hours and days a store is closed.

CD-1 9

☐ 1 CUSTOMER What time do you close? ▸ なんじ

☐ 2 We are open until 7. ▸ しちじ
   • open → 開いている、営業している
           あ   えいぎょう

☐ 3 CUSTOMER From when to when are you open? ▸ えいぎょうじかん

☐ 4 We are open from 10 in the morning until 8 in the evening. / We are open 24 hours a day. ▸ ごぜん

☐ 5 We are open from 10 in the morning until 8 in the evening from Monday to Friday, and on Saturdays we are open from 9 to 7. ▸ げつようび

☐ 6 CUSTOMER On what days is your store closed? ▸ ていきゅうび

☐ 7 Every Monday. / Every third Wednesday. ▸ まいしゅう

☐ 8 We are open every day of the year. ▸ ねんじゅう…
   • every day of the year → 年中
                            ねんじゅう

第1章　敬語の基本パターンと接客の基本表現

"*Nichiyō mo yatte orimasu*" (We are also open on Sundays)

Tips for Working in the Service Industry

"*Yaru*" is also used to mean the same thing as "*ēgyō shiteiru*" and "*aiteiru*". It is a slightly less formal term. Ex) "*Nichiyō mo yattemasu ka?*" "*Hai. Nichiyō mo ēgyō shiteorimasu/yatte orimasu.*"

何時に閉店しますか。
Nan-ji ni hēten shimasu ka?

7時まで開いております。
Shichi-ji made aite orimasu.

営業時間は何時から何時までですか。
Ēgyō jikan wa nan-ji kara nan-ji made desu ka?　　＊営業時間：bussiness hours

午前10時から午後8時まででございます。／24時間営業です。
Gozen jū-ji kara gogo hachi-ji made de gozaimasu. / Nijūyo-jikan ēgyō desu.

月曜日から金曜日までは午前10時から午後8時までで、土曜日は9時から7時までとなっております。
Getsuyōbi kara kin'yōbi made wa gozen jū-ji kara gogo hachi-ji made de, doyōbi wa ku-ji kara shichi-ji made to natte orimasu.

定休日はいつですか。
Tēkyūbi wa itsu desu ka?　　＊定休日：regular holiday

毎週月曜日です。／第3水曜日になります。
Maishū getsuyōbi desu. / Dai-san suiyōbi ni narimasu.

年中無休です。
Nenjūmukyū desu.

31

Unit 9

トイレの案内
Guiding Customers to the Restroom

Memorize expressions used to explain the location of a bathroom inside a store or building.

1 (CUSTOMER) Where is the restroom? ▶ おてあらい

2 Over there, to the back. ▶ あちら
● back → 奥、後ろ

3 At the end of the hallway. ▶ ろうか

4 It's straight down here at the right at the end of the hall. ▶ ここを

5 In the back of the shoe department over there. ▶ あちら
● shoe department → くつ売り場

6 It's outside the store, a little way down to the right. ▶ おみせ
● in a bit → 少し行ったところに

7 Go up the escalator to the second floor. It is to the rear on the left-hand side. ▶ エスカレーター

8 Near the stairs on the first and second floors. ▶ いっかい

Expressing feelings of regret

Tips for Working in the Service Industry

When unable to meet a customer's hopes, instead of simply communicating facts such as "We are not open" or "We do not have any stock," also show your feelings of regret while telling them "*Mōshiwake arimasen.*"(I am very sorry.)

お手洗いはどこですか。
O-tearai wa doko desu ka?　　＊お手洗い：the polite expression of "restroom"

あちらの奥でございます。
Achira no oku de gozaimasu.

廊下の突き当たりでございます。
Rōka no tsukiatari de gozaimasu.

ここをまっすぐ行った突き当たりの右にございます。
Koko o massugu itta tsukiatari no migi ni gozaimasu.

あちらの靴売り場の奥にございます。
Achira no kutsu uriba no oku ni gozaimasu.

お店を出て、右に少し行ったところにございます。
O-mise o dete, migi ni sukoshi itta tokoro ni gozaimasu.

エスカレーターで2階に上がると、左手奥にございます。
Esukarētā de ni-kai ni agaruto, hidarite oku ni gozaimasu.

＊左手奥に：on one's back left

1階と2階の階段付近にございます。
Ikkai to ni-kai no kaidan hukin ni gozaimasu.

＊〜付近：near 〜

Unit 10

よく聞(き)き取(と)れない・わからない
When Something is Hard to Hear / When You Can't Understand

Memorize expressions used when you cannot hear or understand a customer well.

CD-1 11

☐ **1**　Could you please repeat that?
▶ もういちど

☐ **2**　May I ask you to repeat that one more time?
▶ もういちど

☐ **3**　Please wait a bit as I go check.
● check →調(しら)べる、確認(かくにん)する
▶ おしらべします

☐ **4**　Allow me to check. Please wait a moment.
▶ かくにん…

☐ **5**　I'm sorry, I'm unsure of that.
● unsure →わかりかねる
▶ もうしわけ…

☐ **6**　May I ask you to write that here?
▶ ここに

☐ **7**　Please wait a moment, I will get someone else.
● get 〜→〜を呼(よ)んでくる
▶ しょうしょう

"~(Shi) kaneru"

Tips for Working in the Service Industry

"~(Shi) kaneru" means "I would like to do ~, but it is difficult," and is an indirect way of saying that you cannot meet a customer's expectations.

もう一度よろしいですか。
Mō ichido yoroshī desu ka?

もう一度おっしゃっていただけますか。
Mō ichido osshatte itadakemasu ka?

＊おっしゃる：the polite expression of "say"

お調べしますので、しばらくお待ちください。
O-shirabe shimasu node, shibaraku o-machi kudasai.

確認いたしますので、少々お待ちください。
Kakunin itashimasu node, shōshō o-machi kudasai.

申し訳ございません。ちょっとわかりかねます。
Mōshiwake gozaimasen. Chotto wakari kanemasu.

ここに書いていただいてよろしいですか。
Koko ni kaite itadaite yoroshī desu ka?

少々お待ちください。別の者を呼んでまいります。
Shōshō o-machi kudasai. Betsu no mono o yonde mairimasu.

＊～てまいります：the polite expression of "～てくる"

Unit 11

よく使うひとこと表現①
Frequently Used Short Expressions 1

Memorize short expressions frequently used when speaking to customers.

CD-1 12

☐ 1 Understood. ▶ わかり…

☐ 2 Certainly! ▶ かしこまり…

☐ 3 Yes, ma'am. (/ Yes, sir.) ▶ さよう…

☐ 4 That is fine. ▶ けっこう…

☐ 5 That may be difficult.
 • may 〜→〜かと思います、〜かもしれません ▶ それは

☐ 6 I'm sorry, but I cannot do that.
 • can not 〜→〜できかねます、〜できません ▶ もうしわけ…

☐ 7 Is this correct? ▶ よろしい…

☐ 8 Are there any problems? ▶ とくに

"*Kashikomarimashita*" "*Sayō de gozaimasu*"

Tips for Working in the Service Industry

More polite ways of saying "*wakarimashita*" are "*kashikomarimashita/ shōchi itashimashita*", while more polite ways of saying "*sō desu*" ((That) is fine) are "*sayō desu/de gozaimasu*" "*kekkō desu/de gozaimasu.*"

わかりました。
Wakarimashita.

かしこまりました。／承知いたしました。
Kashikomarimashita. / Shōchi itashimashita.

＊承知する : the polite expression of "understood"

左様でございます。
Sayō de gozaimasu.

＊左様 : that's right, yes, so

結構でございます。
Kekkō de gozaimasu.

＊結構 : good, fine

それは難しいかと思います。
Sore wa muzukashī ka to omoimasu.

申し訳ございません。それはちょっとできかねます。
Mōshiwake gozaimasen. Sore wa chotto deki kanemasu.

よろしいでしょうか。
Yoroshī deshō ka?

特に問題はございませんでしょうか。
Tokuni mondai wa gozaimasen deshō ka?

Unit 12

よく使うひとこと表現②
Frequently Used Short Expressions 2

Memorize short expressions frequently used when speaking to customers.

CD-1 13

☐ 1 What would you like to do? ▶ いかが

☐ 2 Please wait a short bit. ▶ しょうしょう

☐ 3 Please wait a moment. ▶ おじかん

☐ 4 Then, I will show you. ▶ では

☐ 5 Is there anything else you're unsure of? ▶ ほかに
  • unsure → 不明な、不確かな
    ふめい　ふたし

☐ 6 Excuse me, has anyone lost an umbrella? ▶ すみません

☐ 7 Excuse me for passing through. ▶ すみません
  • pass through → （前を）通る、通過する
    まえ　　とお　つうか

☐ 8 That is what we ask, though it may be inconvenient. ▶ ごふべん

A single phrase making a large difference

Tips for Working in the Service Industry

"*Mae o shiturē itashimasu.*" (Excuse me for passing in front) is a phrase often used when passing in front of a customer with a cart full of merchandise.

いかがなさいますか。
Ikaga nasaimasu ka?　　　　　　　　　＊いかが : the polite expression of " どう "

少々お待ちください。
Shōshō o-machi kudasai.

お時間、少々いただきます。
O-jikan, shōshō itadakimasu.

では、ご案内いたします。
Dewa, go-annai itashimasu.

ほかに何かご不明な点はございませんでしょうか。
Hokani nanika go-fumē na ten wa gozaimasen deshō ka?　　＊点 : thing, point

---

すみません、どなたか、傘をお忘れではないでしょうか。
Sumimasen, donataka, kasa o o-wasure dewanai deshō ka?

すみません、（ちょっと）前を失礼いたします。
Sumimasen, (chotto) mae o shitsurē itashimasu.
　　　　　　　　　＊失礼いたします : Excuse me, Sorry to bother you

ご不便かもしれませんが、そのようにさせていただいております。
Go-fuben kamo shiremasen ga, sonoyō ni sasete itadaite orimasu.

Unit 13

会計 ①
かいけい

Checking Out 1:
Using a Card

Memorize expressions frequently used when customers are checking out. First, memorize basic expressions used when a credit card is being used.

CD-1 14

☐ 1   You can pay over there.   ▸ おかいけい

☐ 2   How would you like to pay?   ▸ おしはらい

☐ 3   We take credit cards.   ▸ カード

☐ 4   Allow me to take your card.   ▸ カード
• take（→取る、持つ）→預かる
　　　　　と　　も　　　　あず

☐ 5   How many payments would you like this to be?   ▸ おしはらい

☐ 6   Please sign here.   ▸ こちらに

☐ 7   Please input your PIN here.   ▸ こちらに
• input →入力する   • PIN →暗証番号
　　　　にゅうりょく　　　　　　　あんしょうばんごう

☐ 8   Here is your card back as well as your receipt.   ▸ カード

What is the respectful way to say "*suru*"?

Tips for Working in the Service Industry

The "*suru*" in "*dono yō ni suru?*" and "*nan-kai ni suru?*" can be said respectfully by using the term "*nasaru*" (⇒ *~nasaimasu ka?*).

お会計はあちらになります。
O-kaikē wa achira ni narimasu.   　＊会計：payment

お支払いはどのようになさいますか。
O-shiharai wa donoyō ni nasaimasu ka?

カードもお使いになれます。
Kādo mo o-tsukai ni naremasu.   ＊カード：the abbreviation of "credit card"

カードをお預かりします。
Kādo o o-azukari shimasu.

お支払いは何回になさいますか。
O-shiharai wa nan-kai ni nasaimasu ka?

こちらにサインをお願いします。
Kochira ni sain o onegai shimasu.

こちらに暗証番号をご入力ください。
Kochira ni anshōbangō o go-nyūryoku kudasai.

カードのお返しとレシートでございます。
Kādo no o-kaeshi to reshīto de gozaimasu.   ＊お返し：to give it back

Unit 14

会計 ②
かいけい
Checking Out 2: Using Cash

Memorize expressions frequently used when customers pay with cash.

CD-1 15

☐ 1 I'm sorry, but we only take cash. ▶ もうしわけ…

☐ 2 That will be 2,123 yen after tax. ▶ ぜいこみ
- after tax → 税込みで
　　　　　　　ぜいこ

☐ 3 2,000 and 123 yen exactly. ▶ にせん
- exactly → ちょうど

☐ 4 Your total will be 3,955 yen. ▶ おかいけい

☐ 5 From a five thousand yen bill, is that correct? ▶ ごせんえん

☐ 6 From 5,000 yen? Ok. ▶ ごせんえん

☐ 7 Your change is 1,000 and 55 yen. ▶ せん
- change → おつり、お返し
　　　　　　　　　　かえ

☐ 8 Here is your 173 yen back as well as your receipt. ▶ こちら

Things to be careful of when customers are paying with credit cards

Tips for Working in the Service Industry

When receiving a credit card, confirm that you are doing so by saying "*Kādo o o-azukari shimasu.*" (I am taking this card.) Also be sure to check how many payments the customer wishes to make, as some may want to pay over multiple installments.

申し訳ありません。お支払いは現金のみになります。
Mōshiwake arimasen. O-shiharai wa genkin nomi ni narimasu.

＊〜のみ : the formal expression of "only 〜"

税込で 2123 円でございます。
Zēkomi de nisen-hyaku-nijū-san-en de gozaimasu.

2000 と 123 円ですね。ちょうどいただきました。
Nisen to hyaku-nijū-san-en desu ne. Chōdo itadakimashita.

お会計、3955 円になります。
O-kaikē, sanzen-kyūhyaku-gojū-go-en ni narimasu.

5千円からでよろしいでしょうか。
Gosen-en kara de yoroshī deshō ka?

5千円お預かりします。
Gosen-en o-azukari shimasu.

1000 と 55 円のおつりでございます。
Sen to gojū-go-en no otsuri de gozaimasu.

こちら 173 円のお返しと、レシートでございます。
Kochira hyaku-nanajū-san-en no okaeshi to, reshīto de gozaimasu.

Unit 15

会計③
かいけい
Checking Out 3: Other

Memorize other expressions frequently used when customers are checking out.

CD-1 16

1. Do you have an ABC card? ▶ エービーシー…

2. Thank you... Here it is back. ▶ おあずかり…

3. Excuse me. ▶ しつれい…

4. 〈At a restaurant〉
   Will you be paying together? ▶ おかいけい…

5. **CUSTOMER** Separately, please.
   • separately → 別々で、別々に (べつべつ) ▶ べつべつ

6. I apologize for the small change. ▶ おつり

7. **CUSTOMER** Can these gift certificates be used?
   • gift certificates → 商品券 (しょうひんけん) ▶ この

8. Yes. However, we do not give change if these certificates are used, so please be forewarned. ▶ はい

第1章 敬語の基本パターンと接客の基本表現

Ways of paying

Tips for Working in the Service Industry

In Japan, when multiple people are eating out, they may often pay only for themselves and will say something such as "*(Kaikē wa) Betsubetsu de.*"(Please split the check). When customers wish for the bill to be split evenly at izakaya and other locations, they will use the term "*warikan*" (split bill).

ABCカードはお持ちでしょうか。
Ēbīshī kādo wa o-mochi deshō ka?

お預かりします。・・・お返しします。
O-azukari shimasu. .…O-kaeshi shimasu.

失礼しました。
Shitsurē shimashita.

〈レストランなどで〉 お会計はご一緒でよろしいですか。
〈*Resutoran nado de*〉　*O-kaikē wa go-issho de yoroshī desu ka?*

＊一緒（で）：together

 ### 別々でお願いします。
Betsubetsu de onegai shimasu.

おつりが細かくなって申し訳ありません。
Otsuri ga komakaku natte mōshiwake arimasen.

 ### この商品券は使えますか。
Kono shōhinken wa tsukaemasu ka?

はい。ただし、こちらの券の場合、おつりが出ませんので、ご注意ください。
Hai. Tadashi, kochira no ken no bāi, otsuri ga demasen node, go-chūi kudasai.

＊券：ticket, certificate

Unit 16

謝る
あやま
Apologizing

Memorize expressions of apology for when you make a mistake or are unable to respond to a customer's wishes.

CD-1
17

☐ 1 I am sorry. ▸ しつれい

☐ 2 I am very sorry. ▸ たいへん

☐ 3 I apologize for making you wait. ▸ おまたせ…

☐ 4 Thank you for waiting for so long. ▸ たいへん

☐ 5 I apologize for being late. ▸ おそくなって…

☐ 6 Pardon the trouble. ▸ おてすうを…
　　● trouble →お手数／ご面倒／ご迷惑（をかけること）
　　　　　　　てすう　めんどう　めいわく

☐ 7 I am sorry for not being of help. ▸ おやくに…
　　● be of use →役に立つ
　　　　　　　　やく　た

☐ 8 I am truly sorry for causing you trouble. ▸ ごめいわくを

Not "*Gomennasai*", but "*Mōshiwake arimasen*"

Tips for Working in the Service Industry

In customer service settings, "*Gomennasai.*" is never used. Also, instead of "*Sumimasen (deshita).*", the more polite "*Mōshiwake arimasen (deshita)*" is primarily used.

失礼いたしました。
Shitsurē itashimashita.

大変失礼いたしました。
Taihen shitsurē itashimashita.

お待たせして申し訳ありません。
O-mataseshite mōshiwake arimasen.

大変お待たせしました。
Taihen o-matase shimashita.

遅くなってしまい、申し訳ございません。
Osokunatte shimai, mōshiwake gozaimasen.

＊〜てしまう：has a function to express one's regret

お手数をおかけします。／ご面倒をおかけします。
O-tesū o o-kake shimasu. / Go-mendō o o-kake shimasu.

お役に立てず、申し訳ございません。
O-yaku ni tatezu, mōshiwake gozaimasen.

＊〜ず：the formal expression of "〜なくて，〜ないで"

ご迷惑をおかけして、誠に申し訳ありませんでした。
Go-mēwaku o o-kakeshite, makotoni mōshiwake arimasen deshita.

＊誠に：the polite expression of "truly"

The Third Choice
—— "~ ni narimasu"

"*~Ni narimasu*", which means "*~ desu*", is often used in customer service situations, but some may call it "*Baito keigo* (Part-time job respectful language)," and consider it an incorrect phrase. Meanwhile, language experts are growingly accepting the phrase from their professional standpoint as a new form of language usage.

Here are some specific examples.

① こちら、Aセットになります。 (Here is the A set.)
② 受付は10時からになります。 (We begin reception from 10.)
③ 料金は、お一人様1000円になります。
   (The fee is 1,000 yen a person.)
④ こちらは弊社の商品カタログになります。
   (Here is our company's product catalog.)
⑤ 私からの説明は以上になります。
   (That is the explanation from me.)

All of these replace "*~ desu*" or "*~ de gozaimasu*", and it may be preferable in some cases to use those. However, "*~ desu*" lacks politeness, while in other cases "*~ de gozaimasu*" may feel too polite or somewhat stiff. If you would like to avoid declarations while saying something in a soft tone, then "*~ni narimasu*" may be the right term for you.

Though this is often misunderstood, "*~ni narimasu*" is not necessarily used by only younger employees. Elderly individuals also use it, while it is broadly used outside of customer service situations as seen in ④ and ⑤. Words and their usage are such that terms that are initially used incorrectly (or in non-traditional ways) can spread and eventually become accepted as regular usage. This may be a case of such a phenomenon.

第2章

飲食店
いんしょくてん
Restaurant

飲食店の基本①〜⑭／
ファーストフード店①〜③／居酒屋①〜⑤／パブ

Restaurant Basics 1-14 /
Fast Food Stores 1-3 / *Izakaya* 1-5 / Pubs

Unit 1

飲食店の基本①
Restaurant Basics 1: Handling Phone Reservations

Memorize expressions used to communicate desired times and number of seats, as well as corresponding answers.

CD-1 18

☐ 1 (CUSTOMER)	I'd like to make a reservation for five for tonight at seven...	▸ きょうのよるしちじ
☐ 2	Five for seven PM tonight, correct? Certainly.	▸ ほんじつごごしちじ
☐ 3	I'm sorry. We are booked up for six o'clock... • be booked up → 予約でいっぱい / 満席（になっている）	▸ もうしわけありません
☐ 4	I'm sorry. We have a party today, and the entire restaurant is all booked up.	▸ もうしわけありません
☐ 5	I would be able to seat you at seven o'clock.	▸ しちじでしたら
☐ 6 (CUSTOMER)	Do you have any window seats available? / I would like a window seat.	▸ まどぎわのせき
☐ 7	Would it be acceptable if you are not seated together? • be split → （席が）分かれる	▸ おせき
☐ 8	May I ask for your name?	▸ おなまえ

"O-hitori sama"

Tips for Working in the Service Industry

In order to show respect to customers, use "*sama*" when speaking about them using terms such as "*o-kyaku sama*" "*Tanaka sama*", "*3 mē sama*". Even if a customer comes to the store alone, use the phrase "*O-hitori sama de irasshaimasu ka?*" (Are you alone?).

今日の夜7時に5名で予約をしたいのですが……。
Kyō no yoru shichi-ji ni go-mē de yoyaku o shitai no desuga….

＊〜名：the polite expression of "〜人"

本日午後7時に5名様ですね。かしこまりました。
Honjitsu gogo shichi-ji ni go-mē sama desu ne. Kashikomarimashita.

＊本日：the polite expression of "today"

申し訳ありません。6時はご予約でいっぱいなんですが……。
Mōshiwake arimasen. Roku-ji wa go-yoyaku de ippai nan desu ga….

申し訳ありません。本日はパーティーがありまして、貸切になっております。
Mōshiwake arimasen. Honjitsu wa pāthī ga arimashite, kashikiri ni natte orimasu.

＊貸切になっている：be rented out

7時でしたら、お席をご用意できますが。
Shichi-ji deshitara, o-seki o go-yōi dekimasu ga.

窓際の席は空いてますか。／窓際の席がいいのですが。
Madogiwa no seki wa aite masu ka? / Madogiwa no seki ga ī no desu ga.

＊窓際の席：window seat

お席が分かれても、よろしいでしょうか。
O-seki ga wakarete mo, yoroshī deshō ka?

お名前をお伺いしてもよろしいですか。
O-namae o o-ukagai shite mo yoroshī desu ka?

Unit 2

飲食店の基本②
いんしょくてん　きほん
Restaurant Basics 2:
Guiding Visitors 1

Memorize expressions used when customers arrive and they are being shown to their seats.

CD-1 19

☐ **1**　Please sit wherever you would like.　　　　　▶ どうぞ
　　　● sit → おかけください、お座りください

☐ **2**　I'm sorry, these seats are reserved.　　　　　▶ おそれいります

☐ **3**　I will prepare your seats in a moment. Please wait.　　　　　▶ ただいま

☐ **4**　Please purchase food tickets first.　　　　　▶ さきに

☐ **5**　Do you have a reservation?　　　　　▶ ごよやく

☐ **6** (CUSTOMER)　The reservation is for seven o'clock under Kawashima.　　　　　▶ しちじに
　　　● under 〜 → （〜の）名前で

☐ **7**　Allow me to take you to your seat... Here we are.　　　　　▶ おせきへ

☐ **8**　May I take your coat?　　　　　▶ コートを

52

Reception List

Tips for Working in the Service Industry

Some stores may have customers line up and wait when it is crowded, while others have customers write their names on a reception list by the entrance and wait. In the latter case, some customers may write their names on the list and not come back.

どうぞ、お好きな席におかけください。
Dōzo, o-sukina seki ni o-kake kudasai.

恐れ入ります。こちらは予約席になっております。
Osoreirimasu. Kochira wa yoyakuseki ni natte orimasu.

ただ今、お席をご用意しますので、少々お待ちください。
Tadaima, o-seki o go-yōi shimasu node, shōshō o-machi kudasai.

先に食券をお買い求めいただけますか。
Sakini shokken o o-kaimotome itadakemasu ka?

＊食券：food ticket

ご予約を承っておりますでしょうか。
Go-yoyaku o uketamawatte orimasu deshō ka?

7時に川島の名前で予約しています。
Shichi-ji ni Kawashima no namae de yoyaku shite imasu.

お席へご案内いたします。・・・こちらでございます。
O-seki e go-annai itashimasu. ….Kochira de gozaimasu.

コートをお預かりいたしましょうか。
Kōto o o-azukari itashimashō ka?

Unit 3

飲食店の基本③
Restaurant Basics 3: Guiding Visitors 2

Memorize expressions used when confirming customer intentions as they arrive regarding seats and usage time.

☐ **1** We have smoking and non-smoking seats. Which do you prefer?
- smoking seat → 喫煙席
- non-smoking seat → 禁煙席

▶ きんえんせき

☐ **2** I'm sorry, our non-smoking section is full.

▶ もうしわけありません

☐ **3** Do you smoke?

▶ (お)たばこ

☐ **4** I'm sorry, all of our seats are non-smoking.

▶ もうしわけありません

☐ **5** I would be able to seat you at a counter seat immediately, if you don't mind.
- immediately → すぐに

▶ カウンター(せき)

☐ **6** May I seat you together with another party?

▶ ごあいせき

☐ **7** We will be closing in about thirty more minutes, is that alright?

▶ あとさんじゅっぷん

Last Order

Tips for Working in the Service Industry

Thirty minutes to an hour before many restaurants close, they will stop taking any more orders. Going around to customers before this and asking if they have any additional orders is known as "*Rasuto ōdā o toru*"(taking last orders.) Many stores first take last orders for food, and then later for drinks."

禁煙席と喫煙席がございますが、どちらになさいますか。

Kin'en seki to kitsuen seki ga gozaimasu ga, dochira ni nasaimasu ka?

申し訳ありません。禁煙席はいっぱいなんですが。

Mōshiwake arimasen. Kin'en seki wa ippai nan desu ga.

＊いっぱい：be full

（お）たばこはお吸いになりますか。

(O-)tabako wa o-sui ni narimasu ka?

申し訳ありません。全席禁煙になっております。

Mōshiwake arimasen. Zenseki kin'en ni natte orimasu.

＊全席：all seats

カウンター（席）でよろしければ、すぐにご案内できますが。

Kauntā (seki) de yoroshikereba, sugu ni go-annai dekimasu ga.

ご相席になってもよろしいですか。

Go-aiseki ni nattemo yoroshī desu ka?

＊相席：to share a table

あと30分ほどで閉店のお時間になりますが、よろしいでしょうか。

Ato sanjuppun hodo de hēten no o-jikan ni narimasu ga, yoroshī deshō ka?

Unit 4

飲食店の基本④
いんしょくてん　きほん
Restaurant Basics 4: When a Restaurant is Full

Memorize expressions used with customers when a restaurant is full.

CD-1 21

☐ 1　[CUSTOMER] We have a party of three. Will we be able to get in?　▶ さんにん

☐ 2　I'm sorry, we're currently full.　▶ もうしわけありません

☐ 3　[CUSTOMER] How long is the wait?　▶ どれくらい

☐ 4　I believe you will have to wait about twenty to thirty minutes…
　　● you will have to wait → お待ちいただくことになる、お待ちいただかなければならない　▶ にじゅっぷんから

☐ 5　We are very crowded at the moment and it will take about thirty minutes. Is that alright?　▶ たいへん

☐ 6　I'm sorry, but may I ask you to write your name here and wait?　▶ おそれいりますが

☐ 7　Customers will be called in order, so please line up and wait.
　　● in order → 順番に　▶ じゅんばんに

☐ 8　(Mr. / Ms.) Aoki, party of three. Thank you for waiting.　▶ さんめいさま

第2章　飲食店

"O-matase shimashita"

Tips for Working in the Service Industry

"*O-matase shimashita*" is said to any customers who have to wait, even if they did not wait for a particularly long time. It is a phrase commonly said when serving food.

 3人なんですが、入れますか。
San-nin nan desu ga, hairemasu ka?

申し訳ありません。ただ今、満席になっております。
Mōshiwake arimasen. Tadaima, manseki ni natte orimasu.　＊満席：all seats occupied

 どれくらい待ちますか。
Dorekurai machimasu ka?

20分から30分くらいお待ちいただくことになると思いますが……。
Nijuppun kara sanjuppun kurai o-machi itadaku koto ni naru to omoimasu ga….

大変込んでおりまして、30分ほどお時間かかりますが、よろしいでしょうか。　＊〜ほど：the polite expression of "〜about"
Taihen konde orimashite, sanjuppun hodo o-jikan kakarimasu ga, yoroshī deshō ka?

恐れ入りますが、こちらにお名前をお書きになってお待ちいただけますでしょうか。
Osoreirimasu ga, kochira ni o-namae o o-kaki ni natte o-machi itadakemasu deshō ka?
　＊恐れ入りますが〜：the idiomatic phrase when you ask a favor of superior

順番にお呼びしますので、並んでお待ちいただけますか。
Junban ni o-yobi shimasu node, narande o-machi itadakemasu ka?

3名様でお待ちの青木様、お待たせしました。
San-mē sama de o-machi no Aoki sama, o-matase shimashita.

Unit 5

飲食店の基本⑤
Restaurant Basics 5: Taking Orders 1

Memorize expressions used to explain menu items and to confirm orders.

☐ 1 　Here is the menu.
*Here is 〜→（こちらが）〜でございます
▶メニュー

☐ 2 　Today's lunch consists of these three choices.
▶ほんじつの

☐ 3 　The lunch set comes with soup, salad, and a dessert.
▶ランチセット

☐ 4 　This set comes with a pasta of your choice, bread, salad, and a drink. It is a very good deal.
▶こちらの

☐ 5 　Please choose from among these three pastas.
▶パスタは

☐ 6 　I will come back in a moment to take your order.
• in a moment（→すぐに）→のちほど、ただ今
▶のちほど

☐ 7 　Please let me know when you have decided on your order.
▶ごちゅうもん

☐ 8 　Has anyone taken your order?
▶ごちゅうもん

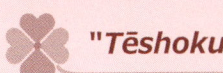

"*Tēshoku*"

Tips for Working in the Service Industry

Items that are combinations of rice and other dishes are known as "*tēshoku*" (Example: *tenpura tēshoku*, *higawari tēshoku* (Daily special)), but items that come with drinks or desserts are not usually known as "*tēshoku*". In these cases, terms such as "*~setto*" and "*~ranchi*" are often used.

メニューでございます。
Menyū de gozaimasu.

本日のランチは、こちらの３種類でございます。
Honjitsu no ranchi wa, kochira no san-shurui de gozaimasu.   ＊種類: kind, sort, type

---

ランチセットには、スープとサラダ、デザートが付いております。
Ranchi setto niwa, sūpu to sarada, dezāto ga tsuite orimasu.

こちらのセットは、お好きなパスタにパンとサラダとドリンクが付いて、大変お得になっております。
Kochira no setto wa, o-suki na pasuta ni pan to sarada to dorinku ga tsuite, taihen o-toku ni natte orimasu.   ＊得になる: to be of benefit

---

パスタはこちらの３つの中からお選びいただきます。
Pasuta wa kochira no mittsu no naka kara o-erabi itadakimasu.

後ほどご注文を伺いに参ります。
Nochihodo go-chūmon o ukagai ni mairimasu.

ご注文がお決まりになりましたら、お呼びください。
Go-chūmon ga o-kimari ni narimashitara, o-yobi kudasai.

ご注文は承っておりますでしょうか。
Go-chūmon wa uketamawatte orimasu deshō ka?

　＊承る: the polite expression when you comply with someone's request

Unit 6

飲食店の基本⑥
(いんしょくてん)(きほん)

**Restaurant Basics 6:
Taking Orders 2**

Memorize questions frequently used when ordering as well as their answers.

CD-1 23

☐ 1 Would you like to order a course, or would you like to order a la carte?   ▶ コース

☐ 2 **CUSTOMER** What do you recommend?   ▶ おすすめ

☐ 3 I recommend the summer vegetable curry.   ▶ こちらの

☐ 4 This cheesecake is our most popular item.   ▶ こちらの

☐ 5 **CUSTOMER** How big is this salad?   ▶ この

☐ 6 It's just right for two people.
  • just right for 〜→〜に（/で）ちょうどいい   ▶ おふたり

☐ 7 Do you have any food allergies?   ▶ なにか

☐ 8 This dish uses no pork.   ▶ この

Being familiar with a store's menu

Tips for Working in the Service Industry

Customers who are coming to a restaurant for the first time will often ask what the store's specialty is. These questions are best answered by introducing the restaurant's most popular items or value-priced items. It is always important to know what is on each menu so that you can give explanations at any time.

コースになさいますか、お好みでご注文なさいますか。
Kōsu ni nasaimasu ka, o-konomi de go-chūmon nasaimasu ka?

＊お好みで：as you please

 おすすめは何ですか。
O-susume wa nan desu ka?

＊おすすめ：recommendation

こちらの夏野菜カレーがおすすめです。
Kochira no natsuyasai karē ga osusume desu.

こちらのチーズケーキが、当店の一番人気です。
Kochira no chīzukēki ga, tōten no ichiban ninki desu.

＊当店：this shop

 このサラダは、どれくらいの量がありますか。
Kono sarada wa dorekurai no ryō ga arimasu ka?

お二人でちょうどいい量だと思います。
O-futari de chōdo ī ryō dato omoimasu.

何か食べ物のアレルギーはございますか。
Nanika tabemono no arerugī wa gozaimasu ka?

このお料理には豚肉は使っておりません。
Kono o-ryōri niwa butaniku wa tsukatte orimasen.

Unit 7

飲食店の基本⑦
Restaurant Basics 7: Taking Orders 3

Memorize expressions used to specifically confirm orders.

CD-1 24

☐ 1 Have you decided on what you would like to order? / May I take your order?
▶ ごちゅうもん

☐ 2 Would you like anything to drink?
• Would you like 〜？→〜はいかがですか。
▶ おのみもの

☐ 3 〈When ordering a set〉
When shall I bring your drink?
▶ おのみもの

☐ 4 Would you like your drink with your meal, or afterwards?
▶ おのみもの

☐ 5 Let me confirm your order.
▶ ごちゅうもん

☐ 6 Let me repeat your order.
▶ ごちゅうもん

☐ 7 Two A sets, one B set, and for drinks, two hot coffees and one iced coffee. Is that correct?
• Is that correct?（→正しいですか）→よろしいですか、お間違いございませんか
▶ エーセットが

☐ 8 Allow me to take your menus.
▶ メニューを

"Sageru"
Tips for Working in the Service Industry

The term "(~o) sageru" is used when taking away a menu or tableware because that customer should be seen as sitting in a high position of respect.

ご注文はお決まりでしょうか。／ご注文をお伺いします。
Go-chūmon wa o-kimari deshō ka? / Go-chūmon o o-ukagai shimasu.

お飲み物はいかがなさいますか。
O-nomimono wa ikaga nasaimasu ka?

〈セットの場合〉お飲み物はいつお持ちしましょうか。
〈setto no bāi〉 O-nomimono wa itsu o-mochi shimashō ka?

お飲み物はお食事と一緒にお持ちしてよろしいでしょうか。それとも、後になさいますか。
O-nomimono wa o-shokuji to issho ni o-mochi shite yoroshī deshō ka? Soretomo ato ni nasaimasu ka?
＊ A それとも B：A or B

ご注文を確認させていただきます。
Go-chūmon o kakunin sasete itadakimasu.

ご注文を繰り返させていただきます。
Go-chūmon o kurikaesasete itadakimasu.

Aセットがお二つ、Bセットがお一つ、お飲み物が、ホットコーヒーがお二つにアイスコーヒーがお一つ。ご注文は以上でよろしいでしょうか。
Ē setto ga o-futatsu, Bī setto ga o-hitotsu, o-nomimono ga, hotto kōhī ga o-futatsu ni aisukōhī ga o-hitotsu. Go-chūmon wa ijō de yoroshī deshō ka?

メニューをお下げします。
Menyū o o-sage shimasu.　　＊（メニューを）下げる：to take away the menu

Unit 8

飲食店の基本⑧
Restaurant Basics 8: Bringing Dishes

Memorize basic expressions used when bringing dishes to tables.

CD-1 25

☐ 1 Thank you for waiting. Here is the tonkatsu meal. ▸おまたせしました

⟨When serving a meal⟩

☐ 2 This is for the customer who ordered the A set. ▸エーセットの

☐ 3 If you would like refills on rice, please let me know. ▸ごはんの

☐ 4 Please be careful, as this is hot. ▸あついので

☐ 5 Please feel free to take your time eating your meal. ▸ごゆっくり
  • to take one's time →ゆっくりする、のんびりする

☐ 6 **CUSTOMER** How do you eat this? ▸これは

☐ 7 This is an already seasoned dish, so please eat it as-is. ▸こちらは
  • as-is, as it is →そのままで

☐ 8 Can I get you anything else? / Will that be everything? ▸ごちゅうもん

Hot dishes

Tips for Working in the Service Industry

When food or vessels containing food such as iron plates are hot, it is kind to warn customers to be careful of the heat.

お待たせしました。とんかつ定食でございます。
O-matase shimashita. Tonkatsu tēshoku de gozaimasu.

＊定食：a set meal

〈料理を差し出すとき〉Ａセットのお客様。
〈ryōri o sashidasu toki〉 Ē setto no o-kyakusama.

ごはんのおかわりは、（お）気軽にお申し付けください。
Gohan no okawari wa, (o-)kigaru ni o-mōshitsuke kudasai.

＊おかわり：another helping　＊気軽に～する：feel free to ～

熱いのでお気をつけください。
Atsui node o-ki o tsuke kudasai.

ごゆっくりお召し上がりください。
Go-yukkuri o-meshiagari kudasai.

これはどうやって食べるんですか。
Kore wa dōyatte taberu n desu ka?

こちらはすでに味が付いておりますので、そのままでお召し上がりください。
Kochira wa sudeni aji ga tsuite orimasu node, sonomama de o-meshiagari kudasai.

ご注文の品はおそろいでしょうか。
Go-chūmon no shina wa o-soroi deshō ka?

Unit 9

飲食店の基本⑨
Restaurant Basics 9: Small Acts of Service

Memorize expressions relating to small acts of service performed while working with customers.

CD-1 26

☐ **1** Would you like a refill of coffee? ▶ コーヒー

☐ **2** Shall I bring individual plates? ▶ とりざら

☐ **3** May I take your empty plates? ▶ あいた

☐ **4** May I take this out of your way? ▶ こちらは

☐ **5** Allow me to bring a child seat. ▶ おこさま

☐ **6** 〈When a customer has ordered a set〉
May I bring you your drink? ▶ おのみもの

☐ **7** Excuse me. Could I move over there? ▶ すみません

☐ **8** Yes, go ahead. I will bring your glass for you... ▶ はい、どうぞ
• go ahead →どうぞ

Allow customers to enjoy their meals

Tips for Working in the Service Industry

For dishes that may be split among multiple people such as salads, prepare individual plates for sharing in advance. Also be sure to quickly take away plates once they are unneeded so that more of the table can be used. If you do not know if a customer is done or not, check by asking "*Kochira wa osumideshō ka.*"(Are you finished with this dish?)

コーヒーのおかわりはいかがですか。
Kōhī no okawari wa ikaga desu ka?

取り皿をお持ちしましょうか。
Torizara o o-mochi shimashō ka?

＊取り皿：a serving plate

空いたお皿をお下げしてもよろしいでしょうか。
Aita o-sara o o-sage shitemo yoroshī deshō ka?

こちらは、お下げしてもよろしいでしょうか。
Kochira wa, o-sage shitemo yoroshī deshō ka.

お子様用のいすをお持ちいたします。
O-ko sama yō no isu o o-mochi itashimasu.

〈セットの場合〉お飲み物をお持ちしてもよろしいでしょうか。
〈*setto no bāi*〉　*O-nomimono o o-mochi shitemo yoroshīdeshō ka?*

すみません、あっちに移ってもいいですか。
Sumimasen, acchi ni utsutte mo ī desu ka?

はい、どうぞ。グラスはこちらでお運びしますので。
Hai, dōzo. Gurasu wa kochira de o-hakobi shimasu node.

＊こちらで〜する：the polite expression of "I /we 〜"

Unit 10

飲食店の基本⑩
Restaurant Basics 10: Making Customers Wait Briefly

Memorize expressions used when customers ask for things, when dishes will be late, and when customers will have to wait.

CD-1 27

☐ 1 CUSTOMER Excuse me, may I see a menu? ▶ すみません

☐ 2 CUSTOMER Excuse me, may I have some water? ▶ すみません

☐ 3 CUSTOMER Excuse me, could you please take this? ▶ すみません
　● take 〜（→〜を持っていく）→〜を下げる

☐ 4 Please wait a moment. ▶ しょうしょう

☐ 5 CUSTOMER Can I sit here? ▶ ここに

☐ 6 Yes, I will clean up this table right away. Please wait a moment. ▶ はい
　● right away →すぐに

☐ 7 CUSTOMER Excuse me, can I order? ▶ すみません

☐ 8 Please wait a moment; I will be right there. ▶ ただいま

Paying attention to the store as a whole

Tips for Working in the Service Industry

While customers often say "*Sumimasen.*" aloud when calling over an employee, sometimes they may instead wave their hands up and not say anything. Always pay attention to the entire store so that you can notice customer voices and signs immediately.

すみません、メニューを見せてもらえますか。
Sumimasen, menyū o misete moraemasu ka?

すみません、お冷をいただけますか。
Sumimasen, o-hiya o itadakemasu ka?　　＊お冷：cold drinking water

すみません、これ、下げてもらえますか。
Sumimasen, kore, sagete moraemasu ka?

少々お待ちください。
Shōshō o-machi kudasai.

ここに座ってもいいですか。
Koko ni suwatte mo ī desu ka?

はい。今、テーブルを片づけますので、少々お待ちください。
Hai. Ima, tēburu o katazukemasu node, shōshō o-machi kudasai.
　　＊片づける：clean up; put something away

すみません、注文いいですか。
Sumimasen, chūmon ī desu ka?

ただいま参りますので、少々お待ちください。
Tadaima mairimasu node, shōshō o-machi kudasai.

Unit 11

飲食店の基本⑪
いんしょくてん　きほん
Restaurant Basics 11:
Changing Orders

Memorize expressions used when dishes are changed or canceled.

CD-1　28

☐ 1　[CUSTOMER] Excuse me, I'd like to change my order. Is that possible?　▶ すみません

☐ 2　Certainly. What would you like?　▶ かしこまりました

☐ 3　[CUSTOMER] I just ordered two coffees. Could you please cancel one of them?　▶ さっき

☐ 4　[CUSTOMER] I just ordered the A lunch, but could you please change it to the B lunch?　▶ さっき

☐ 5　Change your A lunch to a B lunch, correct? Certainly.
   ● 〜, correct? →〜（です）ね。
   　* "ね" has a function to confirm something right or not.　▶ エーランチ

☐ 6　[CUSTOMER] How much longer will it take?　▶ あと

☐ 7　I think I can bring it to you in about ten minutes.　▶ じゅっぷんほど

第2章 飲食店

Don't make careless judgments on your own
Tips for Working in the Service Industry

In situations where you cannot make a judgment such as a customer asking to cancel or change an order, ask the customer to wait while you check. This will not be rude. Panicking and making a judgment on your own may in fact cause trouble in the end. Ask the store manager for his or her instructions.

すみません、注文を変えたいんですが、いいですか。
Sumimasen, chūmon o kaetai n desu ga, ī desu ka?

かしこまりました。いかがなさいますか。
Kashikomarimashita. Ikaga nasaimasu ka?
＊かしこまりました：the polite expression of "I see"

さっきコーヒーを2つ注文したんですが、1つキャンセルしてもらえますか。
Sakki kōhī o futatsu chūmon shita n desu ga, hitotsu kyanseru shite moraemasu ka?
＊さっき：just now

さっきAランチを頼んだんですが、Bランチに変えてもらえますか。
Sakki ē ranchi o tanonda n desu ga, bī ranchi ni kaete moraemasu ka?

AランチをBランチに変更ですね。かしこまりました。
Ē ranchi o bī ranchi ni henkō desu ne? Kashikomarimashita.

あと、どれくらいかかりますか。
Ato, dore kurai kakarimasu ka?

10分ほどでお持ちできるかと思います。
Juppun hodo de o-mochi dekiru ka to omoimasu.
＊〜かと思います：I'm not sure but I think 〜

Unit 12

飲食店の基本⑫
Restaurant Basics 12: Dealing with Complaints

Memorize basic complaints and responses to them.

CD-1 29

□ 1 [CUSTOMER] It looks like there's a bug in this... ▶ あのう

□ 2 I'm sorry. I'll bring a new one out right away. ▶ もうしわけございません
　● bring 〜 out →〜をお持ちする、〜をお出しする

□ 3 [CUSTOMER] Has this fish been cooked all the way? / This looks a little raw. ▶ このさかな

□ 4 I'm sorry. I'll have them make it again right away. ▶ もうしわけございません

□ 5 [CUSTOMER] This glass is dirty right here... ▶ このグラス

□ 6 I'm sorry. I'll get you a new one right away. ▶ もうしわけございません
　● get you a new one →新しいものをお出しする、お取り替えする

□ 7 [CUSTOMER] I didn't order this. / This isn't what I ordered... ▶ これ

□ 8 〈After having made a mistake〉 I'm sorry. ▶ しつれい

Dealing with complaints

Tips for Working in the Service Industry

When dealing with customer complaints, first listen to the customer carefully to understand what the problem is. If it is something that is the store's fault, you will need to sincerely apologize to them as if you made the mistake, even if you didn't make it yourself. In some cases, you may need to immediately report to your supervisor or manager so they can handle the problem.

あのう、中に虫が入ってるみたいなんですが…。
Anō, naka ni mushi ga haitteru mitai na n desu ga….
　＊～みたい（よう）だ：look like ～, seems like ～

申し訳ございません。すぐに新しいものをお持ちします。
Mōshiwake gozaimasen. Suguni atarashī mono o o-mochi shimasu.

この魚、ちゃんと火が通ってるんですか。／これ、ちょっと生焼けっぽいんですが。
Kono sakana, chanto hi ga tōtteru n desu ka? / Kore, chotto namayake ppoi n desu ga.
　＊生焼け：half-roasted, half-raw　＊～っぽい：look like ～, seems like ～

申し訳ございません。すぐに作りなおしてまいります。
Mōshiwake gozaimasen. Suguni tsukuri naoshite mairimasu.
　＊～なおす：to do ～ over again

このグラス、ここが汚れてるんですが……。
Kono gurasu, koko ga yogoreteru n desu ga….

申し訳ございません。すぐにお取り替えいたします。
Mōshiwake gozaimasen. Suguni o-torikae itashimasu.

これ、注文してません。／これ、頼んでないんだけど……。
Kore, chūmon shitemasen. / Kore, tanondenai n da kedo….

〈何かミスをしたとき〉　失礼いたしました。
〈*nanika misu o shita toki*〉　*Shitsurē itashimashita.*

Unit 13

飲食店の基本⑬
Restaurant Basics 13: Dealing with Complaints

Memorize basic complaints and responses to them.

☐ 1 **CUSTOMER** This is different from what I ordered... ▶ これ

☐ 2 I'm sorry. I'll get you a new one right away. ▶ もうしわけございません

☐ 3 **CUSTOMER** I've been waiting for over thirty minutes. How much longer will it be? ▶ もうさんじゅっぷん いじょう

☐ 4 **CUSTOMER** My order isn't coming out at all... ▶ ちゅうもんしたもの

☐ 5 I'm sorry. Your order is being prepared right now, so please wait a little longer. ▶ もうしわけございません

☐ 6 **CUSTOMER** It looks like my order was left out... ▶ じゅんばん

☐ 7 I'm sorry. Let me check on that. ▶ もうしわけございません

It's easier for mistakes to happen when a store is crowded

Tips for Working in the Service Industry

It becomes easier for mistakes to happen when a store is crowded because you have less flexibility. To prevent orders from getting lost, repeat orders that customers have made. Also constantly pay attention to each table to make sure that they are being served.

これ、注文したものと違うんですが……。
Kore, chūmon shita mono to chigau n desu ga….

申し訳ございません。すぐにお取り替えいたします。
Mōshiwake gozaimasen. Suguni o-torikae itashimasu.

もう30分以上待ってるんですが、まだですか。
Mō sanjuppun ijō matteru n desu ga, mada desu ka?

＊まだですか：isn't it ready yet?

注文したものが全然来ないんですが……。
Chūmon shita mono ga zenzen konai n desu ga….

申し訳ございません。ただいまお作りしておりますので、もう少々お待ちください。
Mōshiwake gozaimasen. Tadaima o-tsukuri shite orimasu node, mō shōshō o-machi kudasai.

順番、抜かされているみたいなんですが……。
Junban, nukasareteiru mitai na n desu ga….

＊順番を抜かす：to skip the right order

申し訳ございません。ただいま確認いたします。
Mōshiwake gozaimasen. Tadaima kakunin itashimasu.

Unit 14

飲食店の基本⑭
Restaurant Basics 14: Other

Memorize expressions frequently used prior to closing.

CD-1 31

☐ 1	**CUSTOMER** How late is the restaurant open? • open →営業している	▶おみせは
☐ 2	We are open until ten, and our last order is at nine thirty.	▶じゅうじへいてん
☐ 3	It is the last order for food. Is there anything you would like to order?	▶おしょくじの
☐ 4	The restaurant is very crowded at the moment. Would it be possible to ask you to move? • to move seats →席を移動する	▶てんない
☐ 5	**CUSTOMER** Can leftovers be taken home?	▶のこった
☐ 6	Yes. Allow me to bring you a separate container. • coutainer →容器、入れ物	▶はい
☐ 7	I'm sorry, but we do not allow customers to take food home for food hygiene reasons.	▶おそれいりますが

Bathrooms reflect the store as a whole

Tips for Working in the Service Industry

In general at restaurants, individual employees will be put on bathroom cleaning duty. While some individuals may not have experience cleaning bathrooms other than theirs at home, bathrooms reflect a store as a whole! Be sure to clean them properly.

お店は何時までですか。
O-mise wa nan-ji made desu ka?

10時閉店で、ラストオーダーは9時半です。
Jū-ji hēten de, rasuto ōdā wa ku-ji han desu.

＊閉店：to close the shop

お食事のラストオーダーのお時間ですが、ご注文はいかがなさいますか。
O-shokuji no rasuto ōdā no o-jikan desu ga, go-chūmon wa ikaga nasaimasu ka.

店内が大変込み合ってきましたので、席をお移りいただいてもよろしいでしょうか。
Tennai ga taihen komiatte kimashita node, seki o o-utsuri itadaite mo yoroshī deshō ka?

＊込み合う：to be crowded

残った料理の持ち帰りはできますか。
Nokotta ryōri no mochikaeri wa dekimasu ka?

＊持ち帰り：take-out

はい。では、別の容器にお入れします。
Hai. Dewa, betsu no yōki ni o-ire shimasu.

恐れ入りますが、食品衛生上、お持ち帰りはお断りしております。
Osoreirimasu ga, shokuhin ēsē jō, o-mochikaeri wa o-kotowari shite orimasu.

＊食品衛生：food hygiene　　＊〜上：in terms of 〜, because of 〜

Unit 15

ファーストフード店①

Fast Food Stores 1: Hamburger Shops, Etc. 1

Memorize expressions used when speaking at counters such as at hamburger shops.

☐ 1	Next customer, please.	▶ おつぎ
☐ 2	Will you be eating here or to go? • to go → 持ち帰り	▶ てんない
☐ 3	Here. / To go. CUSTOMER	▶ てんない
☐ 4	〈About a combo / set〉 Please choose one of these for your drink.	▶ おのみもの
☐ 5	The ABC set with the cheeseburger, fries, and the S-size cola. Will that be all?	▶ エービーシー
☐ 6	We have the following limited-time menu.	▶ こちらは
☐ 7	Would you like something to drink?	▶ おのみもの
☐ 8	What size would you like?	▶ サイズ

Use a bright, large voice

Tips for Working in the Service Industry

Speed is demanded in fast food restaurants, so follow the manual and speak established phrases at a good tempo. It is also important to smile and to speak in a bright, loud voice.

お次のお客様、どうぞ。
O-tsugi no o-kyaku sama, dōzo.

店内でお召し上がりですか。お持ち帰りですか。
Tennai de o-meshiagari desu ka? O-mochikaeri desu ka?

店内で。／持ち帰りで。
Tennai de. / Mochikaeri de.

〈セットメニューについて〉
お飲み物はこちらからお選びください。
〈setto menyū ni tsuite〉
O-nomimono wa kochira kara o-erabi kudasai.

ABCセットで、チーズバーガーとポテトのSとコーラ。ご注文は以上でよろしいでしょうか。
Ēbīshī setto de, chīzubāgā to poteto no esu to kōra. Go-chūmon wa ijō de yoroshī deshō ka?　　＊ポテト：French fries　　＊S：an abbreviation of "small size"

こちらは期間限定のメニューでございます。
Kochira wa kikan gentē no menyū de gozaimasu.

お飲み物はいかがですか。
O-nomimono wa ikaga desu ka?

サイズはどちらになさいますか。
Saizu wa dochira ni nasaimasu ka?

Unit 16

ファーストフード店②
Fast Food Stores 2: Hamburger Shops, Etc. 2

Memorize expressions used when speaking at counters such as at hamburger shops.

☐ 1	Would you like fries with that? • fries → （フライド）ポテト	▸ ごいっしょ
☐ 2	Please pay in advance for your meal.	▸ おさき
☐ 3	Can I use this coupon? (CUSTOMER)	▸ この
☐ 4	I'm sorry, this has already expired.	▸ おそれいります
☐ 5	The sugar and milk are over there.	▸ おさとう
☐ 6	Please take this number and wait at your seat.	▸ こちらの
☐ 7	Your number will be called when your order is ready.	▸ できましたら
☐ 8	Customer with number five, thank you for waiting.	▸ 5ばんの

第2章 飲食店

"O-saki ni o-kaikē o ..."

Tips for Working in the Service Industry

The "*o-saki ni*" in 2 means "Before providing the product or service that has been ordered. For example, "*O-saki ni o-kaikē o sasete itadakimasu.*" "*O-saki ni o-kaikē o onegai shimasu.*"(Please pay in advance) is often used.

ご一緒にポテトはいかがですか。
Go-issho ni poteto wa ikaga desu ka?

お先にお会計をお願いしてもよろしいでしょうか。
O-saki ni o-kaikē o onegai shitemo yoroshī deshō ka?

＊先に：in advance

このクーポンは使えますか。
Kono kūpon wa tsukaemasu ka?

恐れ入ります。こちらは有効期限が切れております。
Osoreirimasu. Kochira wa yūkōkigen ga kirete orimasu.

＊有効期限：expiration date

お砂糖とミルクはあちらにございます。
O-satō to miruku wa achira ni gozaimasu.

こちらの番号札をお持ちになって、お席のほうでお待ちください。
Kochira no bangōfuda o o-mochi ni natte, o-seki no hō de o-machi kudasai.

＊番号札：number ticket

できましたら、番号をお呼びいたします。
Dekimashitara, bangō o o-yobi itashimasu.

5番のカードをお持ちのお客様、お待たせいたしました。
Go-ban no kādo o o-mochi no o-kyaku sama, o-matase itashimashita.

Unit 17

ファーストフード店③

Fast Food Stores 3:
Udon, Soba, Beef Bowls, etc.

Memorize expressions used frequently at stores with quick turnover such as udon, soba, and beef bowl chains.

CD-1 34

☐ 1		Which would you like, udon or soba?	▸ うどんとそば
☐ 2		Would you like warm soba or cold soba?	▸ あたたかいそば
☐ 3		We will call your number, so please wait at your seat.	▸ ばんごうで
☐ 4		I'll take your order now.	▸ ごちゅうもん
☐ 5	CUSTOMER	A regular beef bowl, please. / A regular, please. • beef bowl → 牛丼(ぎゅうどん)	▸ ぎゅうどん
☐ 6	CUSTOMER	I'll have a regular beef bowl. / I'll have a regular.	▸ ぎゅうどん
☐ 7	CUSTOMER	Please give me less rice. / Less rice, please.	▸ ごはん
☐ 8	CUSTOMER	A large beef bowl. Less rice, please.	▸ ぎゅうどん

第2章 飲食店

Industry words

Tips for Working in the Service Industry

At beef bowl stores, short phrases are often used when ordering. Focus on memorizing unique phrases and words frequently used by customers in your industry.

うどんとそば、どちらになさいますか。
Udon to soba, dochira ni nasaimasu ka?

温かいそばと冷たいそば、どちらになさいますか。
Atatakai soba to tsumetai soba, dochira ni nasaimasu ka?

番号でお呼びしますので、お席でお待ちください。
Bangō de o-yobi shimasu node, o-seki de o-machi kudasai.

ご注文、どうぞ。
Go-chūmon, dōzo.

牛丼の並、ください。／並、ください。
Gyūdon no nami, kudasai. / Nami, kudasai.

＊並：regular size

牛丼の並で。／じゃあ、並で。
Gyūdon no nami de. / Jā, nami de.

ご飯は少なめにしてください。／ご飯、少なめで。
Gohan wa sukuname ni shite kudasai. / Gohan, sukuname de.

＊少なめ：to be less than the actual amount

牛丼、大盛りで。ご飯、少なめでお願いします。
Gyūdon, ōmori de. Gohan, sukuname de onegaishimasu.

＊大盛り：large serving

第二章 Restaurant

83

Unit 18

居酒屋①
Izakaya 1: Ordering Alcohol 1

Memorize basic expressions relating to alcohol such as drink orders.

☐ **1** May I ask for your drink orders first? ▸ まず

☐ **2** CUSTOMER We'll start with two beers and four glasses. ▸ とりあえず

☐ **3** CUSTOMER Two large draught beers and three mediums.
• draught beer →生ビール
▸ なまビール

☐ **4** Four draught beers, one cola, and one oolong tea. Will that be all? ▸ なまが

☐ **5** CUSTOMER What kind of shochu do you have? ▸ しょうちゅう

☐ **6** We have rice, potato, soba, and barley varieties. ▸ こめ

☐ **7** CUSTOMER I'll have shochu with hot water. ▸ しょうちゅう

☐ **8** CUSTOMER A regular shochu highball and lemon sour shochu highball, please. ▸ ちゅうハイ

第2章　飲食店

Repeating to check

Tips for Working in the Service Industry

Izakaya have large drink menus, and individuals all have their own tastes. You will serve many large groups of customers, so always make sure to repeat orders after they are made to confirm.

まず、お飲み物のご注文をお伺いします。
Mazu, o-nomimono no go-chūmon o o-ukagai shimasu.

とりあえずビール２本とグラスを４つください。
Toriaezu bīru ni-hon to gurasu o yottsu kudasai.

＊とりあえず：first of all　＊ビール２本：two bottled beer

生ビールの大を２つと中を３つください。
Nama bīru no dai o futatsu to chū o mittsu kudasai.

＊大（・中・小）：large (, midium, small)

生が４つ、コーラとウーロン茶がそれぞれ１つ、以上でよろしいでしょうか。
Nama ga yottsu, kōra to ūroncha ga sorezore hitotsu, ijō de yoroshī deshō ka?

＊それぞれ：each one

焼酎は何がありますか。
Shōchū wa nani ga arimasu ka?

＊焼酎：Japanese spirits made from rice/sweet potato /soba/barley.

米、芋、そば、麦、それぞれございます。
Kome, imo, soba, mugi, sorezore gozaimasu.

焼酎のお湯割りをください。
Shōchū no oyuwari o kudasai.

酎ハイとレモンサワーをください。
Chūhai to remon sawā o kudasai.

第二章　Restaurant

85

Unit 19

居酒屋②
(いざかや)

Izakaya 2:
Ordering Alcohol 2

Memorize basic expressions relating to alcohol such as drink orders.

CD-1
36

□ 1 **CUSTOMER** Which has the higher alcohol content, Japanese sake or wine? ▸ にほんしゅ

□ 2 They have about the same alcohol content.
• the same strength →同じくらいの強さ (おな)(つよ)
▸ アルコール

□ 3 The alcohol content of sake is about 15%, red wine is 11 to 14%, and white wine is 7 to 14%. ▸ にほんしゅ

□ 4 Would you like the sake hot or cold? ▸ おさけ

□ 5 **CUSTOMER** Cold, please. ▸ ひや

□ 6 **CUSTOMER** I'd like the sake lukewarm please. ▸ ぬるめ

□ 7 **CUSTOMER** I'll have a glass of red wine. ▸ グラスワイン

□ 8 **CUSTOMER** I'd like to order a bottle of wine. May I see the menu? ▸ ワイン

"*kan*" and "*hiya*"

Tips for Working in the Service Industry

The act of warming alcohol is known as "*kan ni suru*" or "*atsukan ni suru*". Meanwhile, cold drinks are known as "*hiya*". However, both of these words are used almost exclusively with Japanese sake.

日本酒とワインは、どっちのほうがアルコール度数が高いですか。
Nihonshu to wain wa, docchi no hō ga arukōru dosū ga takai desu ka?
＊アルコール度数：strength of alcohol, the alcohol content

アルコール度数は大体同じくらいです。
Arukōru dosū wa daitai onaji kurai desu.

日本酒のアルコール度数が15％くらいで、赤ワインが11〜14％、白ワインが7〜14％です。
Nihonshu no arukōru dosū ga jūgo-pāsento kurai de, akawain ga jūichi kara jūyon-pāsento, shirowain ga nana kara jūyon-pāsento desu.

お酒は熱燗になさいますか、それとも、冷やになさいますか。　*O-sake wa atsukan ni nasaimasu ka, soretomo, hiya ni nasaimasu ka?*
＊熱かん：warmed sake　＊冷や：cold sake

冷やでお願いします。
Hiya de onegai shimasu.

ぬるめの燗でお願いします。
Nurume no kan de onegai shimasu.
＊ぬるめの燗：sake which is warmed as same as human(/room) temprature.

グラスワインの赤をください。
Gurasu wain no aka o kudasai.

ワインをボトルでお願いしたいのですが、メニューを見せてもらえますか。
Wain o botoru de onegai shitai no desu ga, menyū o misete moraemasu ka?

Unit 20

居酒屋③
Izakaya 3: Food Orders and Explaining Food 1

Memorize basic expressions when food is being ordered.

CD-1 37

☐ 1	May I take your food order?	▶ おりょうり
☐ 2	**CUSTOMER** What kind of dish is this?/ What kind of food is this? ● dish → 料理(りょうり)	▶ これは
☐ 3	It is a meat and vegetable stir-fry.	▶ にく
☐ 4	The seasoning is a little spicy.	▶ あじつけ
☐ 5	The dish is fried and seasoned chicken.	▶ あじつけ
☐ 6	It is similar to tempura. ● be similar to 〜 → 〜に似(に)ている	▶ てんぷら
☐ 7	It is a hot pot full of lots of seafood. It will warm you up.	▶ ぎょかいるい
☐ 8	This salad with many ingredients is popular with women.	▶ こちらの

Food words

Tips for Working in the Service Industry

You should learn words that are frequently used when describing food. For example, "*Yaku*"(Grill), "*Ageru*"(Deep fry), "*Itameru*"(Stir fry), "*Yuderu*" (Boil), "*Niru*"(Stew) and more. While "*Yuderu*" means to cook in boiling water, "*Niru*" is used to describe dishes that have been heated in a liquid that is not just water but that also contains seasonings such as soy sauce.

お料理のご注文をお伺いします。
O-ryōri no go-chūmon o o-ukagai shimasu.

これはどんな料理ですか。／これって、どんな料理ですか。
Kore wa donna ryōri desu ka? / Korette, donna ryōri desu ka?

肉と野菜を炒めた料理です。
Niku to yasai o itameta ryōri desu.

＊炒める：to saute

味付けはちょっと辛めです。
Ajitsuke wa chotto karame desu.

味付けした鳥肉を油で揚げた料理です。
Ajitsuke shita toriniku o abura de ageta ryōri desu.

天ぷらに似ています。
Tenpura ni nite imasu.

魚介類がたっぷり入った鍋料理です。体も温まります。
Gyokairui ga tappuri haitta nabe ryōri desu. Karada mo atatamarimasu.

＊たっぷり：generously

こちらの具だくさんのサラダは女性に人気です。
Kochira no gudakusan no sarada wa josē ni ninki desu.

＊具だくさん：full of ingredients

Unit 21

居酒屋④
いざかや

Izakaya 4:
Food Orders and Explaining Food 2

Memorize basic expressions when food is being ordered.

CD-1 38

1. [CUSTOMER] That's all for now. We'll order again later. ▶ とりあえず

2. [CUSTOMER] Is the meat domestic?
   - go well with 〜→〜に（よく）合う

   ▶ おにく

3. Yes. We use high-quality pork from Kagoshima Prefecture. ▶ はい。かごしまけんさん

4. It of course goes well with beer. It goes well with wine, too.
   - domestic →国産（の）こくさん

   ▶ ビールは

5. [CUSTOMER] How many of these are in one serving? ▶ これは

6. I think it's quite a lot, even for a one-person order. ▶ いちにんまえ

7. This assortment is somewhat more of a bargain.
   - assortment →盛り合わせ　●somewhat →少し、多少、いくぶん

   ▶ こちらの

8. You can put lemon juice on it if you like before eating it. ▶ おこのみで

"Moriawase"

Tips for Working in the Service Industry

A "*moriawase*" is a single dish with various things on it. This word is often used with sashimi, ham, cheese, fruit, and so on.

とりあえず以上で。また注文します。
Toriaezu ijō de. Mata chūmon shimasu.　　＊とりあえず : for now, for the present

お肉は国産ですか。
O-niku wa kokusan desu ka?

はい。鹿児島県産の最高級の豚肉を使っております。
Hai. Kagoshima-ken san no saikōkyū no butaniku o tsukatte orimasu.
　　　　　　＊〜産 : from 〜, made in 〜　　＊最高級 : highest class

ビールはもちろん、ワインにもよく合います。
Bīru wa mochiron, wain nimo yoku aimasu.

これは一皿何個ですか。
Kore wa hitosara nan-ko desu ka?

一人前でも、かなりボリュームがあると思います。
Ichi-ninmae demo, kanari boryūmu ga aru to omoimasu.
　　　　　　　　　　　　　＊〜人前 : for 〜 person order

こちらの盛り合わせが少しお得になっております。
Kochira no moriawase ga sukoshi o-toku ni natte orimasu.

お好みでレモンをかけてお召し上がりください。
O-konomi de remon o kakete o-meshiagari kudasai.

Unit 22

居酒屋⑤
(いざかや)

Izakaya 5: Other

Memorize expressions about how to eat dishes, how to take additional orders, and how to explain courses.

CD-1 39

☐ 1 This is soy sauce, while this is thick sauce.
• thick sauce →ソース
▶ こちら

☐ 2 We have Japanese, Chinese, and Italian dressing.
▶ ドレッシング

⟨When a hot pot is heated at the table⟩
☐ 3 It will be ready to eat when the vegetables get soft.
▶ やさいが

☐ 4 Would you like another drink?
▶ おのみもの

☐ 5 Allow me to take your empty glasses.
▶ あいた

☐ 6 Approximately what is your budget?
▶ ごよさん

☐ 7 We also have a 3,000 yen all-you-can-drink course.
• all-you-can-drink：飲み放題
(の) (ほうだい)
▶ さんぜんえん

☐ 8 This 4,000 yen course includes a three-hour all-you-can-drink period.
▶ こちらの

92

Deal with customers properly, even if they are bothersome

Tips for Working in the Service Industry

At an *izakaya*, some customers may try to speak to employees in a familiar way in order to enjoy a conversation. This may annoy you, but you should not show your displeasure or ignore them. Instead, stay professional, don't take offense, and do what needs to be done to complete the interaction.

こちらがしょうゆで、こちらがソースです。
Kochira ga shōyu de, kochira ga sōsu desu.

ドレッシングは和風、中華、イタリアンがございます。
Doresshingu wa wafū, chūka, itarian ga gozaimasu.

〈席で鍋を温めて食べるとき〉
野菜が柔らかくなったら、食べごろです。
〈*seki de nabe o atatamete taberu toki*〉 *Yasai ga yawarakaku nattara, tabegoro desu.*

＊食べごろ：good for eating

お飲み物のおかわりはよろしいでしょうか。
O-nomimono no okawari wa yoroshī deshō ka?

空いたグラスをお下げします。
Aita gurasu o o-sage shimasu.

＊空いたグラス：the glasses having been finished drinking

ご予算はだいたいおいくらでしょうか。
Go-yosan wa daitai o-ikura deshō ka?

3000円の飲み放題コースもございます。
Sanzen-en no nomihōdai kōsu mo gozaimasu.

＊飲み放題コース：the course you can drink as much as you want

こちらの4000円のコースですと、3時間飲み放題になります。
Kochira no yonsen-en no kōsu desuto, san-jikan nomihōdai ni narimasu.

Unit 23

パブ

Pubs:
Ordering Drinks

Memorize basic expressions used when ordering drinks at a pub.

- [ ] 1 **CUSTOMER** I'd like a single of the "Sakura," diluted with water. / I'll have a double of the "Fuji" on the rocks.　　▶「さくら」の

- [ ] 2 **CUSTOMER** I'll have a vodka soda, please.　　▶ ウォッカ

- [ ] 3 **CUSTOMER** Which is easy to drink?　　▶ どれが
  - easy to 〜→〜やすい

- [ ] 4 This has a mild, refreshing taste, and is easy to drink.　　▶ こちらは

- [ ] 5 This does not have much alcohol, so I recommend it to those who can't drink very much .　　▶ アルコール

- [ ] 6 This cocktail is popular with women.　　▶ じょせい

- [ ] 7 Here is the snack menu.　　▶ おつまみ
  - snack →おつまみ

- [ ] 8 **CUSTOMER** I'll have the same thing.　　▶ おなじ

Ways alcoholic beverages are served

Tips for Working in the Service Industry

Alcohol mixed with water is known as "*mizuwari*", while alcohol mixed with soda is known as "*sōda wari*". When spoken as a verb, the form is "*... o mizu de waru.*" (cut it with water.) Something drunk by itself without being mixed with anything is known as "*sutorēto*", while "*rokku/on za rokku*" means it is served with ice only.

🍀 「さくら」のシングルを水割りでお願いします。／「ふじ」のダブルをロックで。
「Sakura」no shinguru o mizuwari de onegaishimasu. /「Fuji」no daburu o rokku de.
＊水割り：diluted with water

🍀 ウォッカのソーダ割りをお願いします。
Wokka no soda wari o onegai shimasu.
＊ソーダ割り：diluted with soda

🍀 どれが飲みやすいですか。
Dore ga nomiyasui desu ka?

こちらはクセがなくさっぱりした味で、飲みやすいです。
Kochira wa kuse ga naku sappari shita aji de, nomiyasui desu.
＊クセがある：having a pequliar flavor　＊さっぱりした：plain, light

アルコールも控えめなので、あまりお酒が強くない方にもおすすめです。
Arukōru mo hikaeme nanode, amari o-sake ga tsuyoku nai kata nimo o-susume desu.

（これは）女性に人気のカクテルです。
(Kore wa) josē ni ninki no kakuteru desu.

おつまみのメニューはこちらでございます。
O-tsumami no menyū wa kochira de gozaimasu.

🍀 同じものをください。
Onaji mono o kudasai.

単語 & ミニフレーズ
Vocabulary + Mini-Phrases

飲食店（いんしょくてん）

塩辛い（しおから）	siokarai / salty	香ばしい（こう）	kōbashī / fragrant
すっぱい	suppai / sour	焼きたて（や）	yakitate / fresh-baked
苦い（にが）	nigai / bitter	新鮮(な)（しんせん）	shinsen(na) / fresh
旨み（うま）	umami / savoriness	食材（しょくざい）	shokuzai / ingredients
あっさりした	assarisita / light	生の（なま）	nama no / raw
こってりした	kotterisita / thick	塩（しお）	shio / salt
味わう（あじ）	ajiwau / to taste	こしょう	koshō / pepper
味わい（あじ）	ajiwai / taste	みそ	miso / miso, bean paste
濃い（こ）	koi / strong	しょうゆ	shōyu / soy sauce
薄い（うす）	usui / thin, weak	だし	dashi / dashi, broth
濃厚(な)（のうこう）	nōkō(na) / rich	にんにく	ninniku / garlic
脂っこい（あぶら）	aburakkoi / fatty	しょうが	shōga / ginger
甘口（あまくち）	amakuchi / sweet	わさび	wasabi / wasabi
辛口（からくち）	karakuchi / spicy	油（あぶら）	abura / oil
たっぷり	tappuri / a lot, plenty	たれ	tare / dipping sauce
歯ごたえ（は）	hagotae / mouthfeel	つゆ	tsuyu / dipping soup
香り（かお）	kaori / fragrance	ソース	sōsu / sauce, Worcestershire sauce
匂い（にお）	nioi / smell		

日本語	ローマ字 / English	日本語	ローマ字 / English
ケチャップ	*kechappu* / ketchup	ピザ	*piza* / pizza
マヨネーズ	*mayonēzu* / mayonnaise	サンドイッチ	*sandoicchi* / sandwich
ドレッシング	*doresshingu* / dressing	トースト	*tōsuto* / toast
からし／マスタード	*karashi/masutādo* / mustard	ハンバーガー	*hanbāgā* / hamburger
唐辛子（とうがらし）	*tōgarashi* / red peppers	フライドポテト	*furaidopoteto* / French fries
トッピング	*toppingu* / toppings	サラダ	*sarada* / salad
硬い（かた）	*katai* / hard	スープ	*sūpu* / soup
柔らかい（やわ）	*yawarakai* / soft	チーズ	*chīzu* / cheese
みそ汁（しる）	*misoshiru* / miso soup	バター	*batā* / butter
刺身（さしみ）	*sashimi* / sashimi, raw fish	ジャム	*jamu* / jam
天ぷら（てん）	*tenpura* / tempura	ビーフ	*bīfu* / beef
マグロ	*maguro* / maguro, tuna	ポーク	*pōku* / pork
サケ	*sake* / salmon	ハム	*hamu* / ham
エビ	*ebi* / shrimp	ソーセージ	*sōsēji* / sausage
貝（かい）	*kai* / shellfish	フルーツ	*furūtsu* / fruit
野菜（やさい）	*yasai* / vegetables	デザート	*dezāto* / dessert
きのこ	*kinoko* / mushrooms	プリン	*purin* / pudding
パスタ	*pasuta* / pasta	ゼリー	*zerī* / jelly

Chapter 2 Restaurant

単語＆ミニフレーズ — 飲食店（いんしょくてん）

シャーベット	*shābetto* sorbet		カロリー	*karorī* calories
ジュース	*jūsu* juice, soft drinks		ダイエット	*daietto* diet
コーラ	*kōra* cola		アレルギー	*arerugī* allergies
カクテル	*kakuteru* cocktail		大盛り（おおも）	*ōmori* large size
炭酸飲料（たんさんいんりょう）／炭酸（たんさん）	*tansan'inryō/tansan* soda water / seltzer water		テイクアウト	*teikuauto* take-out
ミルク	*miruku* milk		名物（めいぶつ）	*meibutsu* famous dish
ガムシロップ	*gamushiroppu* gomme syrup		カフェ	*kafe* café
氷（こおり）	*kōri* ice		喫茶店（きっさてん）	*kissaten* coffee lounge
ストロー	*sutorō* straw		個室（こしつ）	*koshitsu* private room
茶碗（ちゃわん）	*chawan* rice bowl, teacup		座敷（ざしき）	*zashiki* tatami room
湯呑（ゆのみ）	*yunomi* teacup		バイキング	*baikingu* buffet
れんげ	*renge* spoon, china spoon		セルフサービス	*seruhusābisu* self-serve
トレイ	*torē* toilet		宴会（えんかい）	*enkai* banquet
ナプキン	*napukin* napkin		団体客（だんたいきゃく）	*dantaikyaku* large group
おしぼり	*oshibori* wet towel		席が埋まる（せきがうまる）	*seki ga umaru* seats are full
割りばし（わ）	*waribashi* disposable chopsticks		オーダー	*ōdā* order
自家製（じかせい）	*jikasei* homemade		厨房（ちゅうぼう）	*chūbō* kitchen
ヘルシー（な）	*herushī(na)* healthy		シェフ	*shehu* chef

第3章

販売店
Store

販売店の基本①〜⑦／アパレル①〜③／
雑貨店／ドラッグストア①〜④／化粧品店／
スーパー①〜③／家電量販店①〜②

Store Basics 1-7 ／ Apparel 1-6 ／
General Stores ／ Drugstores 1-4 ／ Cosmetics Shop ／
Supermarkets 1-3 ／ Consumer Electronics Retailer 1-2

Unit 1

販売店の基本①
はんばいてん きほん
Store Basics 1:
Simple Phrases Used on Store Floors

Memorize phrases frequently used on store floors to create a store atmosphere.

CD-1 41

☐ 1　Are you looking for something?　　▶ なにか

☐ 2　Please feel free to pick it up.　　▶ どうぞ

☐ 3　Please take your time and look around.　　▶ どうぞ

☐ 4　It is very heavily discounted.　　▶ たいへん

☐ 5　This price includes sales tax.　　▶ こちらは
　　● sales tax → 消費税
　　　　　　　　しょうひぜい

☐ 6　We have other colors as well.　　▶ おいろちがい

☐ 7　Please don't hesitate to let me know if you have any questions.　　▶ なにか
　　● if you have any questions → 何か（お尋ねになりたい
　　　　　　　　　　　　　　　　なに　　　　たず
　　　ことが）ありましたら

☐ 8　Please take this opportunity.　　▶ このきかい

Creating a mood when welcoming a customer

Tips for Working in the Service Industry

When customers enter the store, greet them with a smile to create a comfortable atmosphere. Refrain from having long conversations with other employees or looking bored while working.

何かお探しですか。
Nanika o-sagashi desu ka?

どうぞ、お手にとってご覧ください。
Dōzo, o-te ni totte go-ran kudasai.

＊手にとる：pick up

どうぞ、ごゆっくりご覧ください。
Dōzo, go-yukkuri go-ran kudasai.

大変お安くなっております。
Taihen o-yasuku natte orimasu.

こちらは消費税込みのお値段です。
Kochira wa shōhizē komi no o-nedan desu.

＊〜込み：including 〜

お色違いもございます。
O-irochigai mo gozaimasu.

何かございましたら、お気軽にお声をかけてください。
Nanika gozaimashitara, o-kigaru ni o-koe o kakete kudasai.

＊ございましたら：the polite expression of "ありましたら"

この機会をぜひご利用ください。
Kono kikai o zehi go-riyō kudasai.

Unit 2

販売店の基本②
はんばいてん きほん

Store Basics 2: Products and Services

Memorize expressions used to promote products and services.

CD-1 42

□ 1	This is a new product that went on sale only last month. • go on sale →発売される 　　　　　　　はつばい	▶ こちらは
□ 2	This is one of our store's original products.	▶ こちらは
□ 3	This is a standard stock item with strong popularity. • staple product →定番商品 　　　　　　　ていばんしょうひん	▶ こちらは
□ 4	Everything in the store is now ten percent off.	▶ ただいま
□ 5	We are currently holding a promotion for customers who join.	▶ ただいま
□ 6	I'm sorry, the sale does not apply to this. • not apply to 〜→〜の対象外 　　　　　　　　　たいしょうがい	▶ もうしわけ
□ 7	We are giving away tickets to a drawing for customers who buy a thousand yen or more worth of goods.	▶ せんえん
□ 8	We are giving away small gifts to customers who buy ten thousand yen or more worth of goods. • small gifts →粗品（「つまらない物」ともいう） 　　　　　　そしな　　　　　　　　　もの	▶ いちまんえん

Treating all customers well

Tips for Working in the Service Industry

Once you get used to the job, you may be able to tell the difference between customers who are interested in making a purchase and those who aren't. Even so, customer loyalty can be built by treating all customers in the same way, regardless of the size of their purchases.

こちらは先月発売されたばかりの新商品でございます。
Kochira wa sengetsu hatsubai sareta bakari no shinshōhin de gozaimasu.

こちらは当店のオリジナル商品でございます。
Kochira wa tōten no orijinaru shōhin de gozaimasu.

こちらは定番商品として根強い人気があります。
Kochira wa teiban shōhin toshite nezuyoi ninki ga arimasu.

＊根強い: strongly rooted, deep rooted

ただ今、店内全品が10%オフとなっております。
Tadaima, tennaizenpin ga juppāsento ofu to natte orimasu.

ただ今、入会キャンペーンを行っております。
Tadaima, nyūkai kyanpēn o okonatte orimasu.   ＊入会(する): to become a member

申し訳ございません。こちらはセールの対象外でございます。
Mōshiwake gozaimasen. Kochira wa sēru no taishōgai de gozaimasu.

1000円以上お買い物をされた方に、抽選券を差し上げております。
Sen-en ijō o-kaimono o sareta kata ni, chūsenken o sashiagete orimasu.

＊抽選券: lottery ticket

1万円以上お買い上げの方に、粗品をプレゼントしております。
Ichiman-en ijō o-kaiage no kata ni, soshina o purezento shite orimasu.

Unit 3

販売店の基本③
はんばいてん きほん
Store Basics 3: Stock

Memorize expressions relating to checking stock and putting items on hold.

☐ **1** This product is currently out of stock. ▸ こちらの
  • out of stock →在庫が切れている、在庫切れ
    ざいこ き ざいこぎ

☐ **2** This is the only one of this product we have. ▸ こちらの

☐ **3** I will check our stock. Please wait a moment. ▸ ざいこ

☐ **4** We are currently out of stock, and I will have to back order it for you... ▸ げんざい
  • to back order →お取り寄せをする、取り寄せる
    と よ と よ

☐ **5** The back order will take approximately a week. ▸ おとりよせ

☐ **6** We should be receiving it in two to three days. ▸ に、さんにちちゅう

☐ **7** We will contact you as soon as it's in stock. ▸ しょうひん
  • as soon as 〜→〜次第、〜（する）とすぐに
    しだい

☐ **8** Please fill out this order slip. ▸ こちらの
  • to fill out →記入（する）
    きにゅう

104

Ordering a product

Tips for Working in the Service Industry

When a product is ordered, ask the manufacturer when it can be sent by and confirm with the customer if that is okay. Also confirm their desired color and size once more.

こちらの商品は、現在在庫切れとなっております。
Kochira no shōhin wa, genzai zaikogire to natte orimasu.

こちらの商品は、現品のみとなっております。
Kochira no shōhin wa, genpin nomi to natte orimasu.   ＊現品 : this item (on display)

在庫をお調べしますので、少々お待ちください。
Zaiko o o-shirabeshimasu node, shōshō o-machi kudasai.

現在、在庫切れで、お取り寄せになってしまいますが……。
Genzai, zaikogire de, o-toriyose ni natte shimaimasu ga….

お取り寄せに1週間ほどお時間をいただきます。
O-toriyose ni isshūkan hodo o-jikan o itadakimasu.

2、3日中に入荷する予定でございます。
Ni, san-nichi-chū ni nyūka suru yotē de gozaimasu.

商品が入り次第、ご連絡をさせていただきます。
Shōhin ga hairi shidai, go-renraku o sasete itadakimasu.   ＊連絡をする : to contact

こちらの注文票にご記入をお願いいたします。
Kochira no chūmonhyō ni go-kinyū o onegai itashimasu.

Unit 4

販売店の基本④
はんばいてん きほん
Store Basics 4: Product Packaging

Memorize expressions used at the register relating to product packaging.

CD-1 44

☐ **1** Is this a gift, or is it for your personal use? ▸ こちらは

☐ **2** Shall I gift-wrap this? ▸ ギフトよう
 • gift-wrap → ギフト用に包む
  ようつつ

☐ **3** We charge 200 yen for the box. Is that alright? ▸ おはこだい
 • charge for the (gift) box → お箱代
  はこだい

☐ **4** Would you like the bags separate? ▸ ふくろ

☐ **5** We have three kinds of wrapping paper. Which would you like? ▸ ほうそうよう
 • wrapping paper → 包装用の紙
  ほうそうよう かみ

☐ **6** You can attach a message card. Would you like to do that? ▸ メッセージカード
 • attach → 付ける
  つ

☐ **7** Shall I attach a noshi [ceremonial origami] to the gift? ▸ のし

☐ **8** How is this? ▸ こんな

"Dochira"

Tips for Working in the Service Industry

In general, "*dore*" is used when choosing between three or more options, but more employees have started to use "*dochira*" when they want to be more polite.

こちらは贈り物でしょうか。それともご自宅用でしょうか。

*自宅用: for yourself

Kochira wa okurimono deshō ka? Soretomo go-jitaku-yō deshō ka?

ギフト用にお包みいたしましょうか。

Gifuto-yō ni o-tsutsumi itashimashō ka?

お箱代として200円いただきますが、よろしいでしょうか。

O-hako-dai toshite nihyaku-en itadakimasu ga, yoroshī deshō ka?

袋は別になさいますか。

Fukuro wa betsu ni nasaimasu ka?

包装用の紙は3種類ございますが、どちら（どれ）がよろしいですか。

Hōsō-yō no kami wa san-shurui gozaimasu ga, dochira(dore) ga yoroshī desu ka?

メッセージカードをお付けすることもできますが、いかがなさいますか。

Messējikādo o o-tsuke suru koto mo dekimasu ga, ikaga nasaimasu ka?

のしをお付けしますか。

Noshi o o-tsuke shimasu ka?   *のし: A small decoration placed on things such as gift wrapping paper that is created out of folded colored paper.

こんな感じでよろしいでしょうか。

Konna kanji de yoroshī deshō ka?

Unit 5

販売店の基本⑤
Store Basics 5: Product Shipping

Memorize expressions used when shipping an item.

CD-1 45

☐ 1 　I'd like to send this to Osaka... ▸ これを

☐ 2 　Certainly. Shipping to Osaka will be 780 yen. ▸ かしこまりました

☐ 3 　Shipping charges vary depending on the area to which the item is being shipped. ▸ はいそう
　　　• depending on 〜 → 〜によって

☐ 4 　Do you have a date or time you would like to specify for delivery? ▸ おとどけ

☐ 5 　It will arrive within the week. ▸ いっしゅうかん

☐ 6 　Chilled and frozen foods will incur an extra charge. ▸ れいぞうひん
　　　• incur a charge（→料金（りょうきん）がかかる）→料金（りょうきん）をいただきます

☐ 7 　Could you please write the destination address on this form? ▸ こちらの
　　　• destination address → おとどけ先（さき）

☐ 8 　This is your copy of the receipt. ▸ こちらが

Delivery services

Tips for Working in the Service Industry

Some customers order delivery services as they buy a product, such as when it is being gifted. In such cases, delivery price will change depending on the region and type of product. This is taken into consideration when choosing a product.

 これを大阪に送りたいのですが……。
Kore o Ōsaka ni okuritai no desu ga….

かしこまりました。・・・大阪ですと、送料は780円でございます。
Kashikomarimashita. ….Ōsaka desu to, sōryō wa nanahyaku-hachijū-en de gozaimasu.

＊送料：shipping charges

配送エリアによって料金が異なります。
Haisō eria ni yotte ryōkin ga kotonarimasu.

お届けのお日にちや時間のご指定はございますか。
O-todoke no o-hinichi ya jikan no go-shitē wa gozaimasu ka?

＊お日にち：the polite expression of "date"

１週間以内のお届けになります。
Isshūkan inai no o-todoke ni narimasu.

冷蔵品、冷凍品の場合、追加料金を頂戴いたします。
Rēzōhin, rētōhin no bāi, tsuikaryōkin o chōdai itashimasu.

＊～の場合：in case of ～

こちらの伝票にお届け先をご記入いただけますでしょうか。
Kochira no denpyō ni o-todoke-saki o go-kinyū itadakemasu deshō ka?

こちらが伝票の控えになります。
Kochira ga denpyō no hikae ni narimasu.

Unit 6

販売店の基本⑥
Store Basics 6:
Other, Service at the Register

Memorize expressions used when operating the cash register.

CD-1 46

☐ 1	Next customer to this register, please.	▸ おつぎに
☐ 2	Shall I put that what you are holding together with this in a bag?	▸ そちらの
☐ 3	It is heavy, so I have double-bagged it. • to double bag →袋を二重にする	▸ おもい
☐ 4	[CUSTOMER] Would you like small bags for gift-giving?	▸ おみやげよう
☐ 5	[CUSTOMER] May I have a receipt?	▸ りょうしゅうしょ
☐ 6	Certainly. Should I make it "for payment of goods"? • proviso →ただし書き	▸ かしこまりました
☐ 7	What name shall I write?	▸ おあてな
☐ 8	We look forward to seeing you again.	▸ またの

Receipts

Tips for Working in the Service Industry

Using the word "*reshīto*" in Japan refers to what is printed by a cash register, while saying "*ryōshūsho*" frequently refers to something written by hand on specialized paper. Some receipts have "*ryōshūsho*" printed on them, and these can be submitted to company accounting departments and such.

お次にお待ちのお客様、こちらのレジへどうぞ。
O-tsugi ni o-machi no o-kyaku-sama, kochira no reji e dōzo.

そちらのお荷物も一緒に袋にお入れいたしましょうか。
Sochira no o-nimotsu mo issho ni fukuro ni o-ire itashimashō ka?

重いので、袋を二重にいたします。
Omoi node, fukuro o nijū ni itashimasu.

お土産用に小さい袋を少しいただけますか。
O-miyage-yō ni chīsai fukuro o sukoshi itadakemasu ka?   ＊お土産用：for gift-giving

領収書をお願いします。
Ryōshūsho o onegai shimasu.

かしこまりました。但し書きはお品代でよろしいでしょうか。
Kashikomarimashita. Tadashigaki wa o-shina-dai de yoroshī deshō ka?

お宛名はどうなさいますか。
O-atena wa dō nasaimasu ka?

またのお越しをお待ちしております。
Mata no okoshi o o-machi shite orimasu.   ＊お越し：the polite expression of "coming"

Unit 7

販売店の基本⑦
Store Basics 7: Dealing with Demands for Returns or Lower Prices

Memorize expressions relating to irregular requests from customers such as demands for returns or lower prices.

☐ 1 **CUSTOMER** I got the wrong size so I would like to return this. ▸ サイズ

☐ 2 **CUSTOMER** I'd like to return this for something else... ▸ ほかの

☐ 3 Do you have a receipt? ▸ レシート

☐ 4 Would you like to return it or exchange it? ▸ へんぴん…
 • return (goods) → 返品する

☐ 5 Please understand that items on sale cannot be returned or exchanged. ▸ セールひん
 • items on sale → セール品

☐ 6 **CUSTOMER** Could you make this any cheaper? I'd buy it if it was under 20,000 yen... ▸ これ

☐ 7 **CUSTOMER** I'm over my budget. ▸ よさん
 • budget → 予算

☐ 8 I will speak to my manager. Please wait a moment. ▸ うえのもの

Rules about returns

Tips for Working in the Service Industry

While it is easy to return items in some countries, it is often difficult to return things in Japan unless they are defective. Understand your store's rules regarding returns.

サイズを間違えてしまったので、返品をしたいのですが……。
Saizu o machigaete shimatta node, henpin o shitai no desu ga….

ほかのものと交換したいんですが……。
Hoka no mono to kōkan shitai n desu ga….   ＊交換（する）: to exchange

レシートはお持ちでしょうか。
Reshīto wa o-mochi deshō ka?

返品されますか、それとも、どれかと交換されますか。
Henpin saremasu ka, soretomo, doreka to kōkan saremasu ka?

セール品の場合は、返品や交換には対応いたしかねますので、ご了承ください。
Sēru-hin no bāi wa, henpin ya kōkan niwa taiō itashikanemasu node, go-ryōshō kudasai.   ＊〜いたしかねます: the polite expression of "can not 〜"

これ、もう少し安くなりませんか。２万円を切ったら買うんですが……。
Kore, mō sukoshi yasuku narimasen ka? Niman-en o kittara kau n desu ga….   ＊〜円を切る: become cheaper than 〜 yen

予算をオーバーしているんです。
Yosan o ōbā shiteiru n desu.

上の者と相談してきますので、少々お待ちください。
Ue no mono to sōdan shitekimasu node, shōshō o-machi kudasai.
＊上の者: one's boss/manager

Unit 8

アパレル①

Apparel 1: Suggesting Products

Memorize expressions used to explain and recommend products.

CD-2 / 1

☐ **1** I'm looking for this skirt in this magazine... ▸ この

☐ **2** Do you know what size you normally wear? ▸ おきゃくさま

☐ **3** It's useful to have one of these. ▸ こういうのが
 • useful → 便利(な)、役に立つ

☐ **4** It goes with lots of different clothes, so it is popular with office ladies. ▸ いろいろな

☐ **5** I think it's perfect for formal occasions such as weddings. ▸ けっこんしき

☐ **6** I have one of these as well, and I treasure it. ▸ わたしも
 • treasure 〜 → (〜は)重宝している、〜を大事にしている

☐ **7** This cutsew is very handy for regular use. ▸ こちらの

☐ **8** Wearing it somewhat low cut is the trend this year. ▸ このように

Be careful about your appearance

Tips for Working in the Service Industry

As you are working in a job that involves the sale of clothes, there is a need for you to always be aware of your appearance and outfit. Your shoes are also important, and if you are wearing leather shoes, be sure to have them properly polished.

この雑誌に載っているこのスカートを探しているんですが……。

Kono zasshi ni notteiru kono sukāto o sagashiteiru n desu ga….

お客様の普段のサイズはおわかりですか。

O-kyaku-sama no fudan no saizu wa o-wakari desu ka?

こういうのが一着あると便利だと思います。

Kōiu no ga icchaku aru to benri da to omoimasu.　　＊一着：a suit of clothes

いろいろな服に合わせやすいので、OL に人気があります。

Iroirona fuku ni awaseyasui node, ōeru ni ninki ga arimasu.

＊ OL (Japanese English word)：female office worker

結婚式など、フォーマルな席にぴったりかと思います。

Kekkonshiki nado, fōmaruna seki ni pittari ka to omoimasu.

＊～にぴったり：be perfect for ～

私も一着持っていますが、とても重宝しております。

Watashi mo icchaku motteimasu ga, totemo chōhō shite orimasu.

こちらのカットソーは普段使いにとても便利ですよ。

Kochira no kattosō wa fudan zukai ni totemo benri desu yo.

このように少し浅めにかぶるのが今年のトレンドです。

Konoyōni sukoshi asame ni kaburu no ga kotoshi no torendo desu.

Unit 9

アパレル②

Apparel 2:
Materials

Memorize basic conversational expressions relating to clothing materials.

CD-2 / 2

☐ 1	What kind of material did you want the clothing to be made of?	▶ どのような
☐ 2	What kind of color do you like?	▶ どのような
☐ 3 (CUSTOMER)	What material is this cloth? • cloth → 生地（きじ）	▶ このきじ
☐ 4	It is 50% cotton and 50% polyester.	▶ めん
☐ 5	It lets heat and sweat out, making it cool and comfortable. • let 〜 out →〜を逃がす、〜を外に出す	▶ ねつや
☐ 6	This can be washed in a washing machine, making it easy to care for.	▶ こちらは
☐ 7	You can't wash this in a washing machine, so please take it to a dry cleaners.	▶ せんたくき
☐ 8	This cloth is thin and light but does not let air through, so it's quite warm.	▶ うすくて

Understand trends

Tips for Working in the Service Industry

There are many words to describe materials and colors, as well as types of clothes, and many of the terms are in katakana. Be sure to memorize frequently used terms. Also, always keep an eye out for new trends so that you can speak with customers confidently.

どのような素材のものをお探しですか。
Donoyōna sozai no mono o o-sagashi desu ka?

どのような色がお好みですか。
Donoyōna iro ga o-konomi desu ka?

 この生地の素材はなんですか。
Kono kiji no sozai wa nan desu ka?

綿50％とポリエステル50％でございます。
Men gojuppāsento to poriesuteru gojuppāsento de gozaimasu.

熱や汗を逃がすので、涼しくて気持ちがいいんです。
Netsu ya ase o nigasu node, suzushikute kimochi ga ī n desu.

こちらは洗濯機で洗えますので、お手入れがしやすいです。
Kochira wa sentakuki(sentakki) de araemasu node, o-teire ga shiyasui desu.

＊お手入れ：care and cleaning

洗濯機では洗えないので、ドライクリーニングが必要です。
Sentakuki(sentakki) dewa araenai node, doraikurīningu ga hitsuyō desu.

薄くて軽い生地ですが、風を通さないので、結構暖かいんです。
Usukute karui kiji desu ga, kaze o tōsanai node, kekkō atatakai n desu.

＊風を通す：let air through　＊結構：quite, rather

Unit 10

アパレル③

Apparel 3: Trying Clothes On

Memorize expressions used to speak with customers regarding trying clothes on.

1 There is a mirror over there. ▶ あちら

2 Would you like to try this on?
- try ~ on →~を試着する

▶ ごしちゃく

3 The dressing room is over here. ▶ しちゃくしつ

4 What do you think? ▶ おきゃくさま

5 Is it the right size? / Is it comfortable?
- comfortable →（気持ちがいい→）着心地がいい

▶ サイズ

6 (CUSTOMER) It's a little tight around the waist. ▶ ちょっと

7 I'll bring one that's a size larger. ▶ もうひとつ

8 It looks very good on you.
- look good on ~→~に似合っている

▶ とても

Replying "Īdesu yo." to "Īdesu ka?" is rude

Tips for Working in the Service Industry

You will seem rude if you reply "*Īdesu yo.*"(It's okay.) to a customer asking if it is okay to try on a piece of clothing. Instead, say "*Hai, dōzo.*"(Yes, go ahead.) or "*Mochiron desu.*"(Of course.) In cases where customers ask for permission that cannot be given, instead of saying "*Dame desu.*"(No.), begin by saying "*Mōshiwake gozaimasen ga...*"(I'm sorry, but...) and continue politely by saying "*~ node, ~wa go-enryo itadaite orimasu.*"(because of ~, we ask customers to refrain from ~.)

あちらにお鏡がございます。
Achira ni o-kagami ga gozaimasu.

ご試着なさいますか。
Go-shichaku nasaimasu ka?

試着室はこちらです。
Shichaku-shitsu wa kochira desu.

お客様、いかがでしょうか。
O-kyaku-sama, ikaga deshō ka?

サイズはいかがですか。／着心地はいかがですか。
Saizu wa ikaga desu ka? / Kigokochi wa ikaga desu ka?

＊着心地：feel when worn

ちょっとウエストがきついです。
Chotto uesuto ga kitsui desu.

もう１つ上のサイズをお持ちします。
Mō hitotsu ue no saizu o o-mochi shimasu.

とてもお似合いです。
Totemo o-niai desu.

Unit 11

アパレル ④

Apparel 4: Color / Design

Memorize expressions relating to choosing clothes such as color, design, and size.

☐ 1	**CUSTOMER** Do you have one with this design in a different color? / Do you have this in another color?	▸ おなじ
☐ 2	We have this in navy blue, gray, and khaki.	▸ こちら
☐ 3	We also have this simple type.	▸ こういう
☐ 4	**CUSTOMER** This kind of design doesn't look good on me.	▸ こういう
☐ 5	I think it looks very good on you...	▸ よく
☐ 6	We have three sizes: S, M, L.	▸ エス、エム、エル
☐ 7	Would you like any alterations? • alteration → サイズ直し	▸ サイズ
☐ 8	It will take about an hour to do the alterations.	▸ おなおし

Referring to the elderly

Tips for Working in the Service Industry

There are various terms for referring to the elderly, but one that is not rude in any situation is "*go-nenpai no kata*" (an aged individual). For example, you can use "*Go-nenpai no kata nimo ninki ga arimasu.*" (It is also popular with aged individuals.)

同じデザインで違う色はありますか。／これの色違いはありますか。

Onaji dezain de chigau iro wa arimasu ka? / Kore no irochigai wa arimasu ka?

こちらは紺とグレー、それからカーキ色がございます。

Kochira wa kon to gurē, sorekara kāki iro ga gozaimasu.

こういうシンプルなタイプもございます。

Kōiu shinpuruna taipu mo gozaimasu.

こういう柄は似合わないんです。

Kōiu gara wa niawanai n desu.

よくお似合いだと思いますが……。

Yoku o-niai da to omoimasu ga….

＊〜が…。：An expression used when communicating your feelings or thoughts in a reserved way.

S、M、Lの3つのサイズをご用意しております。

Esu, emu, eru no mittsu no saizu o go-yōi shite orimasu.

＊〜を用意している：have 〜 , make 〜 to be prepared

サイズ直しはされますか。

Saizu naoshi wa saremasu ka?

お直しには1時間ほどかかります。

O-naoshi niwa ichi-jikan hodo kakarimasu.

Unit 12

アパレル⑤

Apparel 5: Shoes

Memorize basic expressions used at shoe stores.

CD-2 / 5

☐ 1 (CUSTOMER) I'm looking for business shoes... ▶ ビジネス…

☐ 2 These are light and good in the rain, making them a popular product. ▶ こちらは
  - be good in the rain → 雨に強い

☐ 3 (CUSTOMER) Do you have them in 25.5 (centimeters)? ▶ にじゅうご…

☐ 4 (CUSTOMER) It's a little tight around my toes. ▶ ちょっと
  - tight → きつい

☐ 5 Would you like me to bring a pair that is a size larger? ▶ では

☐ 6 (CUSTOMER) No, these are narrow at the tip, so I don't think they work with my feet. ▶ いえ
  - tip → 先、つま先

☐ 7 What about this type of shoe? It's slightly wider. ▶ こちら

☐ 8 〈To a female customer〉 Would you like heels that are slightly higher? ▶ もうすこし

Being careful with your words

Tips for Working in the Service Industry

Women are particular about sizes, so be careful when talking about them. For example, tell customers who may be slightly larger that they can wear a certain piece of clothing by saying "*Yuttari shita tsukuri ni natte orimasu.*"(It is made with some slack.) or "*Saizu wa jakkan ōkime ni natte orimasu.*"(It is of a slightly larger size.)

ビジネスシューズを探しているんですが……。
Bijinesu-shūzu o sagashiteiru n desu ga….

こちらは軽くて、雨にも強いので、人気の商品になっております。
Kochira wa karukute, ame nimo tsuyoi node, ninki no shōhin ni natte orimasu.

25.5（センチ）はありますか。
Nijūgo (Nijūgō) ten go (-senchi) wa arimasu ka?

ちょっとつま先のほうがきついんですが……。
Chotto tsumasaki no hō ga kitsui n desu ga….　　＊〜のほう（辺り）: around 〜

では、もうワンサイズ大きいものをお持ちしましょうか。
Dewa, mō wan saizu ōkī mono o o-mochi shimashō ka?

いえ、この靴は先が細くて、私の足には合わないようです。
Ie, kono kutsu wa saki ga hosokute, watashi no ashi niwa awanai yō desu.

こちらのタイプはいかがですか。少し幅が広くなっております。
Kochira no taipu wa ikaga desu ka? Sukoshi haba ga hiroku natte orimasu.

＊幅が広い: wide

〈女性客に〉 もう少しヒールが高いほうがいいでしょうか。
〈Josēkyaku ni〉 Mō sukoshi hīru ga takai hō ga ī deshō ka?

Unit 13

アパレル⑥

Apparel 6:
Bags

Memorize basic expressions used when explaining products at a bag store.

CD-2 6

☐ 1	[CUSTOMER] I'm looking for a business bag to use for commuting to work...	▶ つうきん
☐ 2	This material is waterproof, so it is fine even if it rains.　● be waterproof → 水をはじく	▶ こちらは
☐ 3	This shoulder strap is removable.	▶ こちらの
☐ 4	This bag is made by a well-known Italian manufacturer and is a standard item.	▶ こちらは
☐ 5	[CUSTOMER] I'm looking for a suitcase that's the right size for carry-on baggage on an international flight.　● carry-on ～ → 機内に持ち込める～	▶ かいがいりょこう
☐ 6	This series is light and sturdy, making it perfect for travel.	▶ こちらの
☐ 7	It has pockets on the inside.	▶ うちがわ
☐ 8	It has a simple and elegant design, making it good in formal situations as well.	▶ シンプル

Washing methods

Tips for Working in the Service Industry

Customers frequently ask about how to wash a piece of clothing. Be able to understand and explain the washing instructions printed on the inside of clothes, such as hand washing, machine washing, whole laundering, dry cleaning, ironing, chlorine bleach, shade drying, and more.

 通勤に使うビジネスバッグを探しているんですが……。
Tūkin ni tsukau bijinesu-baggu o sagashite iru n desu ga….

こちらは水をはじく素材なので、雨が降っても大丈夫です。
Kochira wa mizu o hajiku sozai nanode, ame ga futte mo daijōbu desu.

こちらの肩掛けベルトは取り外しができます。
Kochira no katakake beruto wa torihazushi ga dekimasu.

こちらはイタリアの老舗メーカーのバッグで、定番のものです。
Kochira wa Itaria no shinise mēkā no baggu de, tēban no mono desu.

＊老舗：old-established store

海外旅行で機内に持ち込めるサイズのスーツケースを探しています。
Kaigairyokō de kinai ni mochikomeru saizu no sūtsukēsu o sagashite imasu.

＊持ち込む：carry in/on

こちらのシリーズは軽くて丈夫で、旅行や出張に最適です。
Kochira no sirīzu wa karukute jōbu de, ryokō ya shucchō ni saiteki desu.

＊出張：business trip

内側にもポケットが付いています。
Uchigawa nimo poketto ga tsuite imasu.

シンプルで上品なデザインですので、フォーマルな場にもぴったりです。
Shinpuru de jōhinna dezain desu node, fōmaruna ba nimo pittari desu.

Unit 14 雑貨店
General Stores

Memorize expressions used to explain products.

CD-2 7

☐ 1 These mugs come in a two-cup set.
　● mug →マグカップ
　▶ こちらの

☐ 2 This alarm clock allows you to choose from five types of alarm sounds.
　● ～ kinds of A →～種類のA
　▶ こちらの

☐ 3 We also have a pillowcase in the same pattern.
　▶ おなじ

☐ 4 These are all handmade accessories.
　● handmade →手作り（の）
　▶ こちらに

☐ 5 This character is very popular, so we have everything from stationery to lunch boxes and reusable shopping bags featuring it.
　▶ このキャラクター

☐ 6 This stuffed animal is made in Germany, and talks if you press here.
　▶ このぬいぐるみ

☐ 7 [CUSTOMER] It is a very cute pouch, isn't it?
　● pouch →ポーチ
　▶ かわいい

☐ 8 Yes. This is from a series by the popular French brand "Odeon."
　▶ はい

Various products

Tips for Working in the Service Industry

There are many products at general goods stores that make life more fun or convenient. Build your knowledge about your store's products on a daily basis so that you can explain what makes each of them attractive as well as their features.

こちらのマグカップは二つセットになっております。
Kochira no magukappu wa futatsu setto ni natte orimasu.

こちらの目覚まし時計は、5種類の音が選べるようになっております。
Kochira no mezamashi dokē wa, go-shurui no oto ga eraberu yō ni natte orimasu.

同じ柄で枕カバーもございます。
Onaji gara de makura kabā mo gozaimasu.　　　＊枕カバー：pillowcase

こちらにあるのは、すべて手作りのアクセサリーです。
Kochira ni aru nowa, subete tezukuri no akusesarī desu.

このキャラクターはとても人気がありますので、文房具から弁当箱、エコバッグまで、何でもあるんです。
Kono kyarakutā wa totemo ninki ga arimasu node, bunbōgu kara bentōbako, ekobaggu made, nandemo aru n desu.
　　＊文房具（文具）：stationery　　＊エコバッグ：reusable shopping bag

このぬいぐるみはドイツ製で、ここを押すとしゃべるんです。
Kono nuigurumi wa Doitsu-sē de, koko o osuto shaberu n desu.

かわいいポーチですね。
Kawaī pōchi desu ne.

はい。こちらは「オデオン」というフランスの人気ブランドのシリーズです。
Hai. Kochira wa "Odeon" toiu Furansu no ninki burando no shirīzu desu.

Unit 15

ドラッグストア①

Drugstores 1:
Symptoms

Memorize expressions used to confirm a customer's symptoms.

CD-2 8

☐ 1 What are your symptoms?
- symptom → 症状(しょうじょう)
▶ どのような

☐ 2 **CUSTOMER** My stomach feels queasy and I feel like vomiting.
- stomach → 胃(い)   • feel like vomiting → 吐(は)き気(け)がする
▶ いが

☐ 3 **CUSTOMER** I have a terrible cough and can't sleep very well at night.
▶ せきが

☐ 4 Do you have a fever?
▶ ねつは

☐ 5 What kind of pain is it?
▶ どんな

☐ 6 **CUSTOMER** It feels like my head is splitting.
- split → 割(わ)れる
▶ あたまが

☐ 7 **CUSTOMER** 〈Talking about the stomach and abdomen〉
It's a stabbing pain.
▶ さすような

☐ 8 **CUSTOMER** It feels like something is squeezing me tightly.
- squeeze → キューっと締(し)めつける、ギュッと握(にぎ)る
▶ キューっと

What kind of symptoms?

Tips for Working in the Service Industry

It is a good idea to memorize words that are frequently used to describe symptoms.
Gangan: A pain that feels like a loud noise reverberating through the head.
Shikushiku: A word used to describe stomach pain that is not too severe but is a constant unpleasant dull pain.

どのような症状ですか。
Donoyōna shōjō desu ka?

胃がむかむかして、吐き気がするんです。
I ga mukamuka shite, hakike ga suru n desu.　　＊むかむかする：feel queasy

---

咳がひどくて、夜もあまり寝られないんです。
Seki ga hidokute, yoru mo amari nerarenai n desu.　　＊ひどい：terrible

---

熱はありますか。
Netsu wa arimasu ka?

どんな痛みですか。
Donna itami desu ka?

頭が割れるような感じです。
Atama ga wareru yō na kanji desu.

〈胃やお腹など〉刺すような痛みです。
〈*I ya onaka nado*〉 *Sasu yō na itami desu.*　　＊刺す：stab, stick

---

キューっと締め付けられるような感じです。
Kyūtto shimetsukerareru yō na kanji desu.

Unit 16

ドラッグストア②

Drugstores 2: Questions about Medicine

Memorize expressions relating to questions about medicine.

CD-2 9

☐ 1 [CUSTOMER] Can even children take this medicine? ▶ このくすり

☐ 2 Even children can take it as long as they are five or older. ▶ ごさいいじょう
- as long as 〜 → 〜なら、〜であるかぎり
- five or older → 5歳以上

☐ 3 [CUSTOMER] I'm looking for an antidiarrheal medicine... ▶ げりどめ
- antidiarrheal → 下痢止めの

☐ 4 [CUSTOMER] Do you have any good medicine for hayfever? ▶ かふんしょう

☐ 5 This product works for a long time, so many customers buy it. ▶ こちらは

☐ 6 You may feel drowsy after taking this, so please be careful when driving. ▶ くすりを

☐ 7 [CUSTOMER] Do you have cold medicine for children? ▶ こどもよう

☐ 8 This works well on initial cold symptoms such as coughing, sneezing, and runny noses. ▶ こちらは
- work well on 〜 → 〜によく効く

第 3 章　販売店

 Adapting to the environment

Tips for Working in the Service Industry

Depending on the store and time, drug stores may become very crowded. In these cases, another cash register may need to be opened. When this happens, guide customers to the register by saying "*O-tsugi ni o-machi no o-kyaku sama, kochira no reji e dōzo.*" (Next customer, please come to this register.) (⇒ p.115).

 この薬は子どもでも飲めますか。
Kono kusuri wa kodomo demo nomemasu ka?

5歳以上なら、子どもでも飲めます。
Go-sai ijō nara, kodomo demo nomemasu.

 下痢止めの薬が欲しいんですが……。
Geridome no kusuri ga hoshī n desu ga….

 花粉症のいい薬はありませんか。
Kafunshō no ī kusuri wa arimasen ka?

＊花粉症：hay fever

こちらは効果が長く続きますので、買われる方が多いです。
Kochira wa kōka ga nagaku tsuzukimasu node, kawareru kata ga ōi desu.

薬を飲んだ後、眠くなるかもしれませんので、車の運転には気をつけてください。
Kusuri o nonda ato, nemukunaru kamoshiremasen node, kuruma no unten niwa ki o tsukete kudasai.

子ども用の風邪薬はありますか。
Kodomo-yō no kaze-gusuri wa arimasu ka?

こちらは、咳やくしゃみ、鼻水など風邪の初期症状によく効きます。
Kochira wa, seki ya kushami, hanamizu nado, kaze no shokishōjō ni yoku kikimasu.

＊初期症状：initial symptom

131

Unit 17

ドラッグストア③

Drugstores 3: Explaining Medicine

Memorize expressions relating to medicine and how to take it.

☐ 1 These are the tablets. / These are the capsules. ▶ こちらは

☐ 2 This liquid medicine works quickly.
・work quickly → 早く効く、効き目が早い ▶ こちらの

☐ 3 It has very few side effects.
・very few → (〜は) ほとんどない ▶ ふくさよう

☐ 4 Are you allergic to any medication? ▶ くすり

☐ 5 These eye drops work for symptoms from pollen and other allegeries. ▶ このめぐすり

☐ 6 It puts very little strain on your stomach.
・strain → 負担 ▶ いへの

☐ 7 Please take it three times a day after meals.
・after meals → 食後に ▶ いちにち

☐ 8 Please do not take this on an empty stomach. ▶ くうふくじ

Products that sell differ depending on the season

Tips for Working in the Service Industry

Some products may be bought more frequently depending on the season, such as anti-allergy medicine when there is pollen in the spring, bug spray or bug sting calming medicine in the summer, and portable hand warmers in the winter. There are many kinds of these products, so be able to introduce best-sellers as well as the differences between products.

こちらは錠剤でございます。／こちらはカプセルでございます。
Kochira wa jōzai de gozaimasu. / Kochira wa kapuseru de gozaimasu.

こちらの液体の薬は効き目が早いです。
Kochira no ekitai no kusuri wa kikime ga hayai desu.

副作用もほとんどありません。
Fukusayō mo hotondo arimasen.

薬のアレルギーはございますか。
Kusuri no arerugī wa gozaimasu ka?

＊副作用：side effects

この目薬は、花粉などのアレルギー症状にも効果があります。
Kono me-gusuri wa, kafun nado no arerugī shōjō nimo kōka ga arimasu.

胃への負担はほとんどありません。
I eno futan wa hotondo arimasen.

一日３回、食後に服用するようにしてください。
Ichinichi san-kai, shokugo ni fukuyōsuru yō ni shite kudasai.

＊服用する：take a medicine

空腹時には飲まないでください。
Kūfukuji niwa nomanaide kudasai.

＊空腹：being hungry

Unit 18

ドラッグストア ④

Drugstores 4: Other

These are various expressions relating to cosmetics and more that may come up in a drugstore.

CD-2 11

1. I'm looking for sunscreen lotion... ▶ ひやけどめ

2. Is it for use on the face or on the body? ▶ かおよう

3. We recommend this series for individuals with sensitive skin. ▶ びんかんはだ

4. This is the type that does not contain alcohol and is easy on the skin. ▶ アルコール
   - easy on 〜 → 〜にやさしい
   - contain 〜 → 〜を含(ふく)む

5. These cosmetics only use natural ingredients. ▶ てんねん…

6. This medicine requires a prescription, and so we do not carry it. ▶ これは
   - carry → 取(と)り扱(あつか)う、取(と)り扱(あつか)いをする

7. We are offering free samples from Sakura Cosmetics today. ▶ ほんじつ

8. We are offering ten times the normal amount of points today. Please make use of this offer. ▶ ほんじつは
   - make use of 〜 → 〜を利用(りよう)する

"Sarasara" "Shittori"

Tips for Working in the Service Industry

There are many products in drugstores that have to do with hair, known as hair care products. Memorize various words that describe hair condition and product effects such as "*sarasara*" (smooth and dry), "*shittori*" (moist), "*tsuyatsuya*" (shiny), "*uruoi*" (moisture) and "*damēji kea*" (damage care)."

日焼け止めのローションを探しているんですが……。
Hiyakedome no rōshon o sagashiteiru n desu ga….

顔用でしょうか、それともボディ用でしょうか。
Kao-yō deshō ka, soretomo bodhī-yō deshō ka?

敏感肌の方には、こちらのシリーズをお勧めしています。
Binkanhada no kata niwa, kochira no shirīzu o o-susume shite imasu.
＊敏感肌：sensitive skin

アルコールを含まない、肌にやさしいタイプです。
Arukōru o fukumanai, hada ni yasashī taipu desu.

天然成分だけを使った化粧品です。
Tennen sēbun dake o tsukatta keshōhin desu.
＊天然成分：natural ingredients

これは処方せんが必要なお薬で、うちではお取り扱いをしておりません。
Kore wa shohōsen ga hitsuyō na o-kusuri de, uchi dewa o-toriatsukai o shite orimasen.

本日、さくら化粧品の無料サンプルを差し上げております。
Honjitsu, sakura keshōhin no muryō sanpuru o sashiagete orimasu.
＊差し上げる：the polite expression of "offer"

本日はポイントが10倍になります。ぜひご利用ください。
Honjitsu wa pointo ga jū-bai ni narimasu. Zehi go-riyō kudasai.

Unit 19

化粧品店
けしょうひんてん
Cosmetics Shop

Memorize basic expressions about cosmetics frequently used in daily speech.

CD-2 12

☐ 1 **CUSTOMER** I'm looking for a foundation used in the summer. ▶ なつに

☐ 2 This foundation stays on well even if you sweat. ▶ こちらの

☐ 3 This UV-reduction series does a very good job of protecting against ultraviolet rays. ▶ こちらの
   • UV-reduction → UV カット

☐ 4 It prevents wrinkles and spots and even whitens the skin. ▶ シワ
   • wrinckle → シワ   • spot → シミ

☐ 5 **CUSTOMER** Do you have a toner for dry skin? ▶ かんそうはだよう

☐ 6 Toner, milk lotion, and cream are in the set, making it a real bargain. ▶ けしょうすい
   • face lotion → 化粧水 (けしょうすい)   • milky lotion → 乳液 (にゅうえき)

☐ 7 This facial cleanser gets rid of any dirt while also moisturizing very well. I recommend it. ▶ こちらの
   • facial cleanser → 洗顔料 (せんがんりょう)

☐ 8 It will maintain your facial moisture even after you wash your face. ▶ せんがんご

Specialized words are often in katakana

Tips for Working in the Service Industry

Many specialized words are used with cosmetics. Many of these are in katakana, such as "*sukinkea*" (skincare), "*oiru*" (oil), and "*kurīmu*" (cream). There are many ways to say these words, so keep their differences in mind as you learn them.

夏に使うファンデーションを探しているんですが。
Natsu ni tsukau fandēshon o sagashiteiru n desu ga.

こちらのファンデーションは、汗をかいてもお化粧が崩れにくいんです。
*崩れにくい：stay on well
Kochira no fandēshon wa, ase o kaitemo o-keshō ga kuzurenikui n desu.

こちらのUVカットシリーズは、特に紫外線を防ぐ効果の高いものです。
Kochira no yūbui-katto shirīzu wa, tokuni shigaisen o fusegu kōka no takai mono desu.

シワやシミを防ぎ、さらに美白効果もあります。
Shiwa ya shimi o fusegi, sarani bihaku kōka mo arimasu.
*美白：whitening

乾燥肌用の化粧水はありませんか。
Kansōhada-yō no keshōsui wa arimasen ka?

化粧水と乳液、それからクリームがセットになって大変お買い得です。
*(お)買い得：a good deal
Keshōsui to nyūeki, sorekara kurīmu ga setto ni natte taihen o-kaidoku desu.

こちらの洗顔料は、汚れをすっきり落として保湿効果も高いので、おすすめです。
Kochira no senganryō wa, yogore o sukkiri otoshite hoshitsu kōka mo takai node, o-susume desu.

洗顔後も、しっかり肌の潤いを保ってくれます。
Sengan-go mo, shikkari hada no uruoi o tamotte kuremasu.
*(顔の)肌の潤い：facial moisture

Unit 20

スーパー①
Supermarkets 1

Memorize basic expressions often used at the cash register.

CD-2 13

☐ 1 Thank you for waiting. Welcome. ▸ おまたせ…

☐ 2 May I put these in a bag? / Do you need a bag? ▸ ふくろ

☐ 3 Would you like chopsticks? / Shall I include chopsticks? ▸ おはし
 • include →〜を付ける、〜を入れる

☐ 4 Will you need any ice packs? ▸ ほれいざい

☐ 5 Do you have an ABC card? ▸ エービーシーカード

☐ 6 〈Regarding alcohol and cigarettes〉 Please press the age confirmation button on the screen. ▸ がめん

☐ 7 Shall I put these in separate bags? ▸ ふくろ

☐ 8 You can also use these gift certificates. (You will get no change back. Is that all right? ▸ こちら
 • gift certificate → 商品券

Environmentalism

Tips for Working in the Service Industry

When a customer says they do not need a bag, answer with a "*Arigatōgozaimasu.*" (thank you) to let them know that their efforts to preserve the environment are appreciated.

お待たせいたしました。いらっしゃいませ。
Omatase itashimashita. Irasshaimase.

袋にお入れしてよろしいでしょうか。
／袋はご入用でしょうか。
Fukuro ni o-ireshite yoroshīdeshō ka? / Fukuro wa go-iriyō deshō ka?

＊（ご）入用：the polite expression of "need"

お箸はお付けしますか。／お箸をお付けしましょうか。
O-hashi wa o-tsuke shimasu ka? / O-hashi o o-tsuke shimashō ka?

保冷剤はご利用になりますか。
Horēzai wa go-riyō ni narimasu ka?

＊保冷剤：ice pack

ABCカードをお持ちでしょうか。
Ēbīshī kādo o o-mochi deshō ka?

〈酒やタバコについて〉
画面の年齢認証にタッチをお願いいたします。
〈sake ya tabako ni tsuite〉 Gamen no nenrē ninshō ni tacchi o onegai itashimasu.

＊年齢認証：age confirmation

袋は別にいたしますか。
Fukuro wa betsu ni itashimasu ka?

こちらの商品券もご利用になれます。（おつりは出ませんが、よろしいですか。）
Kochira no shōhinken mo go-riyō ni naremasu. (Otsuri wa demasen ga, yoroshī desu ka?)

Unit 21

スーパー②
Supermarkets 2

Memorize basic expressions used when ringing customers up.

1 Your total will be 850 yen.
▶ おかいけい

2 Thank you; 450 yen exactly.
• exactly →ちょうど
▶ よんひゃくごじゅうえん

3 Your change is 550 yen. Please check it.
• make sure 〜 →〜を確かめる
▶ ごひゃくごじゅうえん

4 From 10,000 yen? Ok.
▶ いちまんえん

5 First, here is 9,000 yen in change back.
▶ おさきに

6 And here is the remaining 250 yen.
• remaining 〜→残りの〜、(お)後の〜
▶ おあと

7 Thank you very much. Please come again.
▶ ありがとう…

Don't speak quickly

Tips for Working in the Service Industry

Once you get used to a job, you will find yourself saying frequently-used words such as "*Arigatōgozaimashita.*"(thank you) and "*Mata o-koshi kudasaimase.*"(please come again) naturally. However, if these are said quickly, it will be difficult to hear them. Say these with sincerity and work hard to make sure they can be properly heard.

お会計、850円でございます。
O-kaikē, happyaku gojū-en de gozaimasu.

450円ちょうどいただきます。
Yon'hyaku gojū-en chōdo itadakimasu.

550円のお返しでございます。お確かめください。
Gohyaku gojū-en no o-kaeshi de gozaimasu. O-tashikame kudasai.

＊(お)返し：change

1万円お預かりいたします。
Ichiman-en o-azukari itashimasu.

＊預かる：keep, receive

お先に9000円のお返しでございます。
O-saki ni kyūsen-en no o-kaeshi de gozaimasu.

＊お先に：first

お後、250円のお返しでございます。
O-ato, nihyaku gojū-en no o-kaeshi de gozaimasu.

ありがとうございました。またお越しくださいませ。
Arigatōgozaimashita. Mata o-koshi kudasaimase.

＊越す：the polite expression of "来る"

Unit 22

スーパー ③
Supermarkets 3

Memorize basic expressions regarding where products are placed and discounts.

CD-2 15

☐ 1 Excuse me, where is the pepper? ▶ すみません

☐ 2 It is on that top shelf over there. ▶ あちらの

☐ 3 I'm sorry, this product is limited to one per customer. ▶ おそれいります
- one per customer → お一人様お一つ(ひとりさま　ひと)

☐ 4 All prices include tax. ▶ かかく
- price → 価格、値段(かかく　ねだん)

☐ 5 Is this the price after discount? ▶ これ

☐ 6 No, this is the price before discount. The discount will be deducted at the register. ▶ いえ
- register → レジ

☐ 7 I'm sorry. Today's special sold out this morning. ▶ おそれいります

☐ 8 We will be offering a limited-time sale beginning at 5 PM. ▶ このあと
- limited-time sale → タイムセール

Informing customers of locations

Tips for Working in the Service Industry

Supermarkets are large, so when a customer asks where an item is, tell them "*Go-annai itashimasu.*" (allow me to show you) and guide them close to the correct location. Some elderly individuals will not be able to see prices well, either.

 すみません、こしょうはどこにありますか。
Sumimasen, koshō wa doko ni arimasu ka?

あちらの棚の上段にございます。
Achira no tana no jōdan ni gozaimasu.   ＊棚の上段 : the top of the shelf

恐れ入ります。こちらの商品は、お一人様お一つとさせていただいております。
Osoreirimasu. Kochira no shōhin wa, o-hitori-sama o-hitotsu to sasete itadaite orimasu.

価格はすべて税込でございます。
Kakaku wa subete zēkomi de gozaimasu.

 これは値引き後の価格ですか。
Kore wa nebiki go no kakaku desu ka?   ＊値引き : discount

いえ、こちらは値引き前の価格です。レジにてお値引きさせていただきます。
Ie, kochira wa nebiki mae no kakaku desu. Reji nite o-nebiki sasete itadakimasu.

恐れ入ります。本日の特売品は午前中に売り切れてしまいました。
Osoreirimasu. Honjitsu no tokubaihin wa gozenchū ni urikirete shimaimashita.

＊特売品 : special

この後、17時からタイムセールを行います。
Konoato, jūshichi-ji kara taimusēru o okonaimasu.

Unit 23

家電量販店① (かでんりょうはんてん)
Consumer Electronics Retailer 1

Memorize basic expressions relating to explanations of consumer electronics.

CD-2 16

☐ 1	This is the newest model. • newest →最新の(さいしんの)、いちばん新しい(あたらしい)	▶ こちら
☐ 2	The features are considerably better than before.	▶ じゅうらいより
☐ 3	The picture quality is even better than previous models.	▶ じゅうらいモデル
☐ 4	It is easy to operate. • to operate →操作(そうさ)（する）	▶ そうさ
☐ 5	It is easily detachable, making repairs easy. • detachable →とりはずせる	▶ かんたんに
☐ 6	It is compact and handy to carry around.	▶ コンパクトで
☐ 7	These two have essentially the same performance.	▶ このふたつ
☐ 8	This consumes little power so it allows you to save on your electric bill.	▶ こちらは

第3章 販売店

 Knowledge about products

Tips for Working in the Service Industry

Be able to explain what makes products unique, such as their features, convenient qualities, capabilities, design, price, cost of use, and after-sale service. However, keep in mind that customers value different elements to different degrees.

こちらは最新の機種でございます。
Kochira wa saishin no kishu de gozaimasu.

＊機種：model

従来より機能が格段によくなっております。
Jūrai yori kinō ga kakudan ni yoku natte orimasu.

＊機能：function, feature

従来のモデルに比べ、画質がさらにきれいになっております。
Jūrai no moderu ni kurabe, gashitsu ga sarani kirē ni natte orimasu.

操作も簡単です。
Sōsa mo kantan desu.

簡単に取り外せるので、お手入れも楽です。
Kantan ni torihazuseru node, o-teire mo raku desu.

コンパクトで、持ち運びにも便利です。
Konpakuto de, mochihakobi nimo benri desu.

＊持ち運び：bringing around

この二つは、性能はほとんど変わりません。
Kono futatsu wa, sēnō wa hotondo kawarimasen.

＊性能：performance

こちらは消費電力が少ないので、電気代を節約できます。
Kochira wa shōhidenryoku ga sukunai node, denki-dai o setsuyaku dekimasu.

＊消費電力：power consumption

145

Unit 24

家電量販店②
かでんりょうはんてん
Consumer Electronics Retailer 2

Memorize basic expressions relating to product warranties and customer service.

CD-2 17

1 Delivery and installation is free.
- delivery → 配送（はいそう）
- installation → 設置（せっち）

▸ はいそう

2 It is difficult to discount this product, but we can reduce the price with points.

▸ こちらの

3 I can also add a three-year extended warranty.
- extended warranty → 延長保証（えんちょうほしょう）

▸ さんねんかん

4 This is within the warranty period, so it will be repaired for free.

▸ しょうきかん…

5 I'm sorry, but this is no longer in the warranty period, so we will have to ask you to pay for repair costs.

▸ おそれいりますが

6 This requires replacement parts, but it is an old model and the parts themselves seem to no longer be made.
- no longer 〜 → もう〜ない

▸ ぶひん

7 If there is anything you don't understand about its use, please call this customer center.

▸ おつかい

8 This is a toll-free number for customers.

▸ おきゃくさま

Product quality guarantees

Tips for Working in the Service Industry

Product guarantees are generally given by manufacturers, not stores, but be sure to tell customers of their guarantee period when they are buying a product.

配送と設置の費用は無料です。
Haisō to secchi no hiyō wa muryō desu.

こちらの商品はお値引きが難しいのですが、ポイントで還元することができます。
Kochira no shōhin wa o-nebiki ga muzukashī no desu ga, pointo de kangen suru koto ga dekimasu.

＊還元する：reduce, give back, give in return

３年間の延長保証をお付けすることもできます。
San-nenkan no enchōhoshō o o-tsuke suru koto mo dekimasu.

保証期間内ですので、無料で修理させていただきます。
Hoshōkikan-nai desunode, muryō de shūri sasete itadakimasu.

＊期間内：within the period

恐れ入りますが、保証期間が切れておりますので、修理代はお客様負担になります。
Osoreirimasu ga, hoshōkikan ga kirete orimasu node, shūri-dai wa o-kyaku-sama futan ni narimasu.

部品の交換が必要なんですが、型が古くて、部品自体をもう作っていないそうなんです。
Buhin no kōkan ga hitsuyō na n desu ga, kata ga furukute, buhin jitai o mō tsukutteinai sō na n desu.

＊交換：replacement　　＊部品：parts

お使いになって、もしわからないことがあったら、こちらのカスタマーセンターにお電話ください。
O-tsukai ni natte, moshi wakaranai koto ga attara, kochira no kasutamāsentā ni o-denwa kudasai.

お客様専用のフリーダイヤルです。
O-kyaku-sama senyō no furīdaiyaru desu.

単語 & ミニフレーズ
Vocabulary + Mini-Phrases

販売店 (はんばいてん)

日本語	ローマ字／英語
木綿 (もめん)	*momen* / cotton
絹／シルク (きぬ)	*kinu/shiruku* / silk
麻 (あさ)	*asa* / linen, hemp
ウール	*ūru* / wool
カシミヤ	*kashimiya* / cashmere
アクリル	*akuriru* / acrylic
革 (かわ)	*kawa* / leather
長袖 (ながそで)	*nagasode* / long-sleeve
半袖 (はんそで)	*hansode* / short-sleeve
七分袖 (しちぶそで)	*shichibusode* / three-quarter sleeve
ノースリーブ	*nōsurību* / sleeveless
Vネック	*buinekku* / v-neck
丸首 (まるくび)	*marukubi* / round-necked
タンクトップ	*tankutoppu* / tank top
タートルネック	*tātorunekku* / turtleneck
スーツ	*sūtsu* / suit
ジャケット	*jaketto* / jacket
シャツ	*shatsu* / shirt
ワイシャツ	*waishatsu* / dress shirt
Tシャツ	*thīshatsu* / T-shirt
ワンピース	*wanpīsu* / one-piece dress
ブラウス	*burausu* / blouse
セーター	*sētā* / sweater
カーディガン	*kādhigan* / cardigan
コート	*kōto* / coat
靴下 (くつした)	*kutsushita* / socks
ストッキング	*sutokkingu* / stockings
インナー／下着 (したぎ)	*innā/shitagi* / underwear
赤 (あか)	*aka* / red
青 (あお)	*ao* / blue
黄色 (きいろ)	*kīro* / yellow
緑 (みどり)	*midori* / green
ピンク	*pinku* / pink
オレンジ	*orenji* / orange
茶色 (ちゃいろ)	*chairo* / brown
紫 (むらさき)	*murasaki* / purple

水色 みずいろ	mizuiro aqua blue	手袋 てぶくろ	tebukuro gloves
ベージュ	bēju beige	帽子 ぼうし	bōshi hat
グレー／灰色 はいいろ	gurē/haiiro gray	サングラス	sangurasu sunglasses
紺 こん	kon navy blue	指輪 ゆびわ	yubiwa ring
ＬＬサイズ	eruerusaizu XL / LL-size	イヤリング	iyaringu earring
ハンドバッグ	handobaggu handbag	ピアス	piasu piercing
リュックサック ／デイパック	ryukkusakku/ deipakku backpack	ネックレス	nekkuresu necklace
巾着 きんちゃく	kinchaku pouch	口紅 くちべに	kuchibeni lipstick
スニーカー	sunīkā sneakers	アイシャドウ	aishadō eye shadow
サンダル	sandaru sandals	チーク	chīku blush
パンプス	panpusu pumps	フェイスパウダー	feisupaudā face powder
ハイヒール	haihīru high heels	マニキュア	manikyua manicure
ブーツ	būtsu boots	乳液 にゅうえき	nyūeki milky lotion
マフラー	mafurā muffler / scarf	専門店 せんもんてん	senmonten specialty shop
スカーフ	sukāfu scarf	リニューアル	rinyūaru renovation / renewal
ハンカチ	hankachi handkerchief	新発売 しんはつばい	shinhatsubai new product
ネクタイ	nekutai necktie	ヒット商品 しょうひん	hittoshōhin hit product
		ブーム	būmu popular

単語＆ミニフレーズ — 販売店（はんばいてん）

日本語	ローマ字 / English
ディスカウント	*dhisukaunto* — discount
バーゲン	*bāgen* — bargain sale
特価（とっか）	*tokka* — special price
高級（こうきゅう）	*kōkyū* — luxury
ブランド	*burando* — brand
ブランド品（ひん）	*burandohin* — brand goods
国産（こくさん）	*kokusan* — domestically-made
オリジナル	*orijinaru* — original
（ご）贈答用（ぞうとうよう）	*(go-)zōtōyō* — as a present
お中元とお歳暮（ちゅうげん と せいぼ）	*o-chūgen to o-sēbo* — A custom of exchanging gifts during certain periods in the summer and winter in order to express your daily feelings of gratitude.
冷凍食品（れいとうしょくひん）	*reitōshokuhin* — frozen foods
乳製品（にゅうせいひん）	*nyūsēhin* — dairy products
シリアル	*shiriaru* — cereal
レトルト食品（しょくひん）	*retorutoshokuhin* — sterile packaged foods
缶詰（かんづめ）	*kanzume* — canned
ベビー用品（ようひん）	*bebīyōhin* — baby products
調味料（ちょうみりょう）	*chōmiryō* — seasoning
小麦粉（こむぎこ）	*komugiko* — flour
サラダ油（ゆ）	*saradayu(abura)* — salad oil
食パン（しょく）	*shokupan* — white bread
惣菜（そうざい）	*sōzai* — side dish
ペットフード	*pettofūdo* — pet food
ペットボトル	*pettobotoru* — plastic bottle
洗剤（せんざい）	*senzai* — detergent
シャンプー	*shanpū* — shampoo
リンス	*rinsu* — rinse
コンディショナー	*kondhishonā* — conditioner
歯磨き（はみがき）	*hamigaki* — toothpaste
消臭剤（しょうしゅうざい）	*shōshūzai* — deodorant
殺虫剤（さっちゅうざい）	*sacchūzai* — insecticide
トイレットペーパー	*toirettopēpā* — toilet paper
電球（でんきゅう）	*denkyū* — light bulb

第4章

コンビニ
Convenience Stores

コンビニ①〜⑤

Convenience Stores 1-5

Unit 1

コンビニ①

Convenience Stores 1: Registers 1

Memorize basic expressions used when ringing someone up at a cash register.

CD-2 18

☐ 1 Next customer, please. ▸ つぎの

☐ 2 Shall I put this in a bag? / Will you need a bag?
● bag → 袋(ふくろ)
▸ ふくろ

☐ 3 Would you like to take it as-is?
● as-is → このまま
▸ このまま

☐ 4 One 108 yen item and one 216 yen item for a total of 324 yen for two items. ▸ ひゃくはちえん

☐ 5 〈When there is change〉
From 1,000 yen? Ok.
▸ せんえん

☐ 6 Your change is 676 yen. Please make sure it's correct.
● make sure → 確(たし)かめる
▸ ろっぴゃくななじゅう

☐ 7 〈When no change is needed.〉
324 yen exactly.
▸ さんびゃくにじゅう…

☐ 8 Here is your receipt. ▸ こちら

Giving customers change

Tips for Working in the Service Industry

Handing a customer change at a cash register using only one hand will give off a rude impression. Hold the money in one hand while accompanying it with your other hand as you give a customer change.

次のお客様（お次の方）、どうぞ。
Tsugi no o-kyaku-sama (O-tsugi no kata), dōzo.

袋にお入れしてよろしいですか。／袋はご利用でしょうか。
Fukuro ni o-ireshite yoroshīdesu ka? / Fukuro wa go-riyōdeshō ka?

このままでよろしいですか。
Konomama de yoroshīdesu ka?   *〜がいい、〜でいい : would like 〜

108円が1点、216円が1点、合計2点で324円頂戴いたします。
Hyaku-hachi-en ga itten, nihyaku-jūroku-en ga itten, gōkē ni-ten de sanbyaku-nijūyo-en chōdai itashimasu.   *〜点 : 〜 item, 〜 piece

---

〈おつりがある場合〉　1000円お預かりいたします。
〈*Otsuri ga aru bāi*〉　*Sen-en o-azukari itashimasu.*

676円のお返しです。お確かめください。
Roppyaku-nanajūroku-en no o-kaeshi desu. O-tashikame kudasai.

〈おつりがない場合〉　324円ちょうどいただきます。
〈*Otsuri ga nai bāi*〉　*Sanbyaku-nijūyo-en chōdo itadakimasu.*

こちら、レシートでございます。
Kochira, reshīto de gozaimasu.

Unit 2

コンビニ②

Convenience Stores 2: Registers 2

Memorize expressions used in situations such as when a customer pays with a large bill.

 CD-2 19

⟨When there is one item⟩

□ 1　Your total is 1,080 yen. / 1,080 yen, please.　▶ おかいけい
　　• total（→合計）→（お）会計

□ 2　From 5,000yen? Ok.　▶ ごせんえん

□ 3　First, here are your bills back. One thousand, two thousand, three thousand yen. Please make sure it's correct.　▶ さきに

□ 4　And here is the remaining 920 yen. Please make sure it's correct.　▶ おあと
　　• remaining 〜→残りの〜、(お)後の〜

⟨From a 10,000 yen bill⟩

□ 5　First, here are your bills back. Five thousand, six thousand, seven thousand, eight thousand yen. Please make sure it's correct.　▶ さきに

□ 6　And here is the remaining change, 920 yen, as well as your receipt.　▶ おあと

□ 7　Thank you very much. Please come back again.　▶ ありがとう…

Say things aloud to prevent mistakes

Tips for Working in the Service Industry

When taking or returning money, say the corresponding amount of money, such as "~ en o-azukarishimasu." (From ~ yen? Ok.) and "~en no o-kaeshi desu." (Here is ~ yen back) to keep from making mistakes.

〈商品が一つの場合〉お会計、1080円でございます。／1080円頂戴いたします。
〈shōhin ga hitotsu no bāi〉 O-kaikē, sen-hachijū-en de gozaimasu. / Sen-hachijū-en chōdai itashimasu.

5千円お預かりいたします。
Gosen-en o-azukari itashimasu.

先に大きい方から千、二千、三千円のお返しです。お確かめください。
Sakini ōkī hō kara sen, nisen, sanzen-en no o-kaeshi desu. O-tashikame kudasai.

＊大きい方：bills ⇔ 細かい方（small change）

お後、920円のお返しです。お確かめください。
O-ato, kyūhyaku-nijū-en no o-kaeshi desu. O-tashikame kudasai.

〈1万円からの場合〉先に大きい方から五千、六千、七千、八千円のお返しです。お確かめください。
〈Ichiman-en kara no bāi〉 Sakini ōkī hō kara gosen, rokusen, nanasen, hassen-en no o-kaeshi desu.

お後、細かい方、920円のお返しと、レシートでございます。
O-ato, komakai hō, kyūhyaku nijū-en no o-kaeshi to, reshīto de gozaimasu.

ありがとうございました。またお越しくださいませ。
Arigatōgozaimashita. Mata o-koshi kudasai mase.

Unit 3

コンビニ ③

Convenience Stores 3:
Registers 3

Memorize expressions used when customers pay with a card.

CD-2 20

- [ ] 1 I want to pay by credit card, please. ▸ カード

- [ ] 2 You seem to be 85 yen short. What would you like to do? ▸ はちじゅうごえん
  • short → 不足している
  　　　　　 ふそく

- [ ] 3 Would you like to charge it? ▸ チャージ

- [ ] 4 I'd like to charge 2,000 yen to the card. ▸ にせんえん

- [ ] 5 ⟨When a card is being read⟩
  Please touch your card against the surface. ▸ タッチ

- [ ] 6 ⟨After charging a card⟩
  Please try again. / Please touch the card [on the reader] one more time. ▸ もういちど

- [ ] 7 ⟨After charging a card⟩
  Please pay for your transaction now. ▸ おしはらい

- [ ] 8 I'll pay with cash, then. ▸ じゃあ

第4章 コンビニ

Dealing with various customers

Tips for Working in the Service Industry

Some customers may have quiet voices that are hard to hear, while others may be wearing headphones and listening to music. Look at a customer to see how they are acting and deal with them patiently.

 カードでお願いします。
Kādo de onegai shimasu.

85円不足しておりますが、いかがなさいますか。
Hachijūgo-en fusoku shite orimasu ga, ikaga nasaimasu ka?

＊いかが（＝どう）：how, what

チャージなさいますか。
Chāji nasaimasu ka?

 2000円、チャージをお願いします。
Nisen-en, chāji o onegai shimasu.

（読み取り部に）タッチをお願いします。
(Yomitori-bu ni) Tacchi o onegai shimasu.

〈チャージの後〉もう一度お願いします。
／もう一度タッチしていただけますか。
〈*Chāji no ato*〉 *Mō ichido onegai shimasu. / Mō ichido tacchi shiteitadakemasu ka?*

〈チャージの後〉続けてお支払い、お願いします。
〈*Chāji no ato*〉 *Tsuzukete o-shiharai, onegai shimasu.*

＊続けて：(and) then, (and) now

 じゃあ、現金で払います。
Jā, genkin de haraimasu.

Unit 4

コンビニ ④

Convenience Stores 4: Food and Drink

Memorize expressions often used when customers are purchasing food.

CD-2 21

☐ **1** Would you like this to be heated? ▶ こちら

☐ **2** Would you like chopsticks? / Shall I include chopsticks? ▶ おはし
  - include → （付ける→）お付けする

☐ **3** Will one pair of chopsticks be enough? ▶ おはし

☐ **4** ⟨About coffee⟩
Which would you like, hot or iced? ▶ ホット

☐ **5** What size of coffee would you like? ▶ コーヒー

☐ **6** Shall I bag your hot and cold items separately? ▶ あたたかい

☐ **7** ⟨For oden⟩
How much broth would you like with that? / How much broth shall I put in? ▶ おしる

Giving consideration to customer age and sex

Tips for Working in the Service Industry

When elderly individuals buy pasta, they may prefer chopsticks over a fork, so be sure to ask them, "*O-hashi o o-tsuke shimasu ka, fōku o o-tsuke shinasu ka?*" (Would you like a fork or would you like chopsticks?) Be able to deal with customers appropriately given their age and sex.

こちらは温めますか。
Kochira wa atatamemasu ka?

お箸はお付けしますか。／お箸をお付けしましょうか。
O-hashi wa o-tsuke shimasu ka? / O-hashi o o-tsuke shimashō ka?

お箸は１膳でよろしいでしょうか。
O-hashi wa ichi-zen de yoroshī deshō ka?

＊膳：the counter suffix for chopsticks

（コーヒーは）ホットとアイス、どちらになさいますか。
(Kōhī wa) Hotto to aisu, dochira ni nasaimasu ka?

コーヒーのサイズはどちらになさいますか。
Kōhī no saizu wa dochira ni nasaimasu ka?

温かい物と冷たい物、袋は別々に致しますか。
Atatakai mono to tsumetai mono, fukuro wa betsubetsu ni itashimasu ka?

〈おでんの場合〉お汁はどれくらいお入れしますか。／（お）つゆはどれくらいお入れしますか。
〈oden no bāi〉 O-shiru wa dorekurai o-ire shimasu ka? / (O-)tsuyu wa dorekurai o-ire shimasu ka?

＊（お）つゆ：soup of Oden

Unit 5

コンビニ⑤

Convenience Stores 5:
Deliveries and Copies

Memorize expressions used when accepting parcels or about copy services.

CD-2 22

☐ 1 I'd like to have this package delivered... ▶ これ

☐ 2 Do you have a shipping slip?
 ● shipping slip → 伝票 (でんぴょう) ▶ でんぴょう

☐ 3 Will you pay here, or will the delivery be COD?
 ● pay here → 元払い (もとばらい) ● COD → 着払い (ちゃくばらい) ▶ もとばらい

☐ 4 Please fill this out. ▶ こちら

☐ 5 This is your copy.
 ● copy → 控え (ひかえ) ▶ こちら

☐ 6 〈When returning part of a payment for a public services bill〉
This is yours to keep. ▶ こちら

☐ 7 Copies are self-service. ▶ コピーき

☐ 8 Please put money into the copier to operate it. ▶ コピーき

Where to wait in line

Tips for Working in the Service Industry

Many individuals use convenience stores, and there are often times where the store will be temporarily crowded. All stores indicate where to wait in line, but be careful as this information may sometimes be hard to understand.

 これ、宅配に出したいんですが……。
Kore, takuhai ni dashitai n desu ga….　　＊宅配(便)：door-to-door delivery service

---

伝票はお持ちでしょうか。
Denpyō wa o-mochi deshō ka?

元払いか着払い、どちらになさいますか。
Motobarai ka chakubarai, dochira ni nasaimasu ka?

こちらにご記入ください。
Kochira ni go-kinyū kudasai.

こちら、お客様の控えでございます。
Kochira, o-kyaku-sama no hikae de gozaimasu.

〈公共料金の支払いで、書類の一部を返すとき〉
こちら、お返しいたします。
〈kōkyōryōkin no shiharai de, shorui no ichibu o kaesu toki〉
Kochira, o-kaeshi itashimasu.

コピーはセルフサービスになっております。
Kopī wa serufusābisu ni natte orimasu.

コピー機はコインを入れてお使いください。
Kopī-ki wa koin o irete o-tsukai kudasai.

単語＆ミニフレーズ
Vocabulary + Mini-Phrases

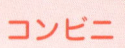
コンビニ

日本語	ローマ字 / English
おにぎり	*onigiri* / rice ball
お弁当	*o-bentō* / lunch box
肉まん	*nikuman* / meat bun
から揚げ	*karaage* / fried chicken nugget
コロッケ	*korokke* / croquette
メンチカツ	*menchikatsu* / mincemeat croquette
カップ麺	*kappumen* / instant noodles
ヨーグルト	*yōguruto* / yogurt
チョコレート	*chokorēto* / chocolate
アイスクリーム	*aisukurīmu* / ice cream
ミネラルウォーター	*mineraruwōtā* / mineral water
缶ビール	*kanbīru* / canned beer
ポケットティッシュ	*pokettothisshu* / pocket tissues
マスク	*masuku* / cold mask
カイロ	*kairo* / hand warmer
電池	*denchi* / batteries
充電器	*jūdenki* / recharger
チケット	*chiketto* / ticket
写真のプリント	*shashin no purinto* / printed photo
公共料金	*kōkyōryōkin* / public utilities charge
電気代	*denkidai* / electricity bill

第5章

宿泊施設
Accommodations

宿泊施設①〜⑥

Accommodations 1-6

Unit 1

宿泊施設①
しゅくはくしせつ

Accommodations 1:
Taking Reservations on the Phone 1

Memorize expressions used to confirm the number of nights and room type.

CD-2 23

☐ 1   Thank you for calling. This is Sakura Hotel.   ▶ おでんわ

☐ 2   [CUSTOMER] I'd like to make a reservation.   ▶ よやく

☐ 3   When will the reservation be for?   ▶ なんにち

☐ 4   [CUSTOMER] From March 15.   ▶ さんがつ

☐ 5   How many nights are you planning to stay?   ▶ なんぱく
  • how many nights 〜？→何泊〜？
  なんぱく

☐ 6   How many guests?   ▶ なんめい…

☐ 7   What type of room would you like?   ▶ どのような

☐ 8   [CUSTOMER] A single, and I'd prefer a non-smoking room…   ▶ シングル

第5章　宿泊施設

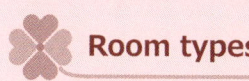
Room types

Tips for Working in the Service Industry

Words to describe room types such as "*shinguru*" (single) or "*tsuin*" (twin) may be used in different ways outside of Japan. Pay attention and confirm you know what they mean.

お電話ありがとうございます。さくらホテルでございます。

O-denwa arigatōgozaimasu. Sakura hoteru de gozaimasu.

 予約をお願いしたいのですが。

Yoyaku o onegaishitai no desu ga.

何日のご予約でしょうか。

Nan-nichi no go-yoyaku deshō ka?

 3月15日からなんですが。

San-gatsu jūgo-nichi kara na n desu ga….

何泊のご予定でしょうか。

Nan-paku no go-yotē deshō ka?

何名様でしょうか。

Nan-mē-sama deshō ka?

＊〜名様：the polite expression of "〜人"

どのようなお部屋をご希望でしょうか。

Donoyōna o-heya o go-kibō deshō ka?

 シングルで、禁煙の部屋がいいんですが……。

Shinguru de kin'en no heya ga ī n desu ga….

Unit 2

宿泊施設②
しゅくはくしせつ

Accommodations 2:
Taking Reservations on the Phone 2

Memorize expressions used to complete reservations, such as explaining accommodation fees, names, and addresses.

CD-2 24

☐ **1** The accommodation fee will be 6,500 yen including tax. ▶ しゅくはくりょうきん
- accommodation fee → 宿泊料金（しゅくはくりょうきん）

☐ **2** I'm sorry, but all of our singles are full. ▶ もうしわけありませんが
- full → いっぱいの、満室の（まんしつ）

☐ **3** A smoking room is available, however... ▶ きつえん

☐ **4** We have rooms available on the seventeenth... ▶ じゅうしちにち
- opening → (部屋の) 空き（へや・あ）

☐ **5** May I ask for your name and phone number? ▶ おなまえ

☐ **6** Check-in begins at three. ▶ チェックイン

☐ **7** May I ask what time you plan to check in? ▶ チェックイン

☐ **8** Thank you for your reservation on June 15 of a single room for one night. ▶ ではろくがつ…

第5章　宿泊施設

 Begin by putting the customer at ease

Tips for Working in the Service Industry

When a problem arises and a customer calls from their room, repeat what they are saying while confirming the situation. Then tell them that a staff member will be by their room in (x) minutes to put the customer at ease.

宿泊料金は税込みで 6500 円でございます。
Shukuhaku ryōkin wa zēkomi de rokusen gohyaku-en de gozaimasu.

申し訳ありませんが、シングルはいっぱいでございます。
Mōshiwakearimasen ga, shinguru wa ippai de gozaimasu.

喫煙のお部屋ならお取りできますが……。
Kitsuen no o-heya nara o-tori dekimasu ga….

＊（部屋を）取る：reserve (a room)

---

17 日なら空きがございますが……。
Jūshichi-nichi nara aki ga gozaimasu ga….

お名前とお電話番号をいただけますか。
O-namae to o-denwa bangō o itadakemasu ka?

チェックインは3時からになります。
Chekkuin wa san-ji kara ni narimasu.

チェックインのご予定時間をお伺いできますか。
Chekkuin no go-yotējikan o o-ukagai dekimasu ka?

＊伺う：the polite expression of "ask"

では6月15日、シングルご1泊でご予約を承りました。
Dewa roku-gatsu jūgo-nichi, shinguru go-ippaku de go-yoyaku o uketamawarimashita.

Chapter 5 Accommodations

167

Unit 3

宿泊施設 ③
しゅくはくしせつ

Accommodations 3: Checking in

Memorize interactions at the front desk when customers check in.

CD-2 25

☐	1 CUSTOMER	My name is Tanaka, and I have a room reserved for one night starting today.	▶ きょうから
☐	2	Mr. Tanaka? Please wait a moment.	▶ たなかさま
☐	3	Please write your name and address here.	▶ では
☐	4	Your room number is 506. Here is your room key.	▶ おへや
☐	5	Here is your breakfast voucher. • breakfast voucher → 朝食券 ちょうしょくけん	▶ こちら
☐	6	Breakfast is served at the Sakura restaurant on the first floor.	▶ ちょうしょく
☐	7	Please go up to the fifth floor using that elevator.	▶ あちら
☐	8	Your room will be on the right after you get off the elevator. • on the right → 右手に、右側に みぎて みぎがわ	▶ おへや

Emergency exits and escape routes

Tips for Working in the Service Industry

While Japan is a country blessed with beautiful nature, it also has many natural disasters. Be sure to know exactly where emergency exists and escape routes are.

 今日から1泊で予約している田中です。
Kyō kara ippaku de yoyaku shiteiru Tanaka desu.

田中様ですね。少々お待ちください。
Tanaka-sama desu ne. Shōshō o-machi kudasai.

では、こちらにお名前とご住所をお書きください。
Dewa, kochira ni o-namae to go-jūsho o o-kaki kudasai.

お部屋の番号は506です。こちらがお部屋の鍵でございます。
O-heya no bangō wa go-zero-roku desu. Kochira ga o-heya no kagi de gozaimasu.

こちらが朝食券でございます。
Kochira ga chōshokuken de gozaimasu.

朝食は1階のレストラン「さくら」でご用意します。
Chōshoku wa ikkai no resutoran "Sakura" de go-yōi shimasu.

＊（朝食を）用意する：prepare (breakfast), get (breakfast) ready

あちらのエレベーターで5階までお上がりください。
Achira no erebētā de go-kai made o-agari kudasai.

お部屋はエレベーターを降りられて、右手にございます。
O-heya wa erebētā o orirarete, migite ni gozaimasu.

＊降りられる：the polite form of "降りる"

Unit 4

宿泊施設④
Accommodations 4: SOS from Rooms

Memorize internal calls from rooms informing you of an SOS.

1. Yes, this is the front desk. / Thank you for waiting. This is the front desk. ▶ はい

2. **CUSTOMER** There's no hot water coming out of the shower... ▶ シャワー

3. **CUSTOMER** The toilet isn't flushing...
   ● flush → （水が）流れる ▶ トイレ

4. **CUSTOMER** The air conditioning isn't working.
   ● work → 効く、動く ▶ エアコン

5. I understand, sir. We will send someone right away.
   ● send (someone) → （だれかを）行かせる ▶ かしこまりました

6. **CUSTOMER** I don't understand how to use the remote control. ▶ リモコン

7. **CUSTOMER** The window isn't opening... ▶ まど

8. I will be there right away. ▶ すぐに

"O-matase shimashita. ~ desu."

Tips for Working in the Service Industry

When answering in the phone in Japan, the phrase "*Hai, ~ desu.*" is generally used. If you could not pick up the phone immediately, use "*O-matase shimashita. ~ desu.*" (*Only in work situations)."

はい、フロントです。／お待たせしました。フロントです。
Hai, furonto desu. / Omatase shimashita. Furonto desu.

シャワーのお湯が出ないんですが……。
Shawā no o-yu ga denai n desu ga….

トイレの水が流れないんですが……。
Toire no mizu ga nagarenai n desu ga….

エアコンが効かないんですが……。
Eakon ga kikanai n desu ga….

かしこまりました。すぐに係の者を行かせます。
Kashikomarimashita. Suguni kakari-no-mono o ikasemasu.

＊係の者：the person in charge to the matter

リモコンの使い方がわからないんですが……。
Rimokon no tsukaikata ga wakaranai n desu ga….

窓が開かないんですが……。
Mado ga akanai n desu ga….

すぐにお伺いします。
Suguni o-ukagai shimasu.

＊伺う：the polite expression of "go (to where someone is)"

Unit 5

宿泊施設⑤
しゅくはくしせつ

Accommodations 5: Requests from Rooms

Memorize expressions used to request items or services as well as responses to them.

CD-2 27

☐ 1 **CUSTOMER** I'd like to borrow another blanket if possible... ▸ もう

☐ 2 Certainly. One will be brought up right away.
- be brought up（→持ってこられる）
  → （係の者が）お持ちします
  かかりもの　　も
▸ かしこまりました

☐ 3 **CUSTOMER** The room next to mine is noisy... ▸ となりの

☐ 4 I'm sorry. I can move you to a different room. Would you like to do that? ▸ もうしわけございません

☐ 5 **CUSTOMER** The room smells like cigarettes. Can I change rooms?
- smell like cigarettes →タバコのような匂いがする、
  にお
  タバコくさい
▸ へやが

☐ 6 Allow me to show you to another room. ▸ べつの

☐ 7 **CUSTOMER** Could you please call me a taxi? ▸ タクシーを

☐ 8 Certainly. When will you be leaving? ▸ かしこまりました

Changing rooms

Tips for Working in the Service Industry

Complaints requesting that a room be changed are not uncommon. While it is best if a room can be changed, the situation will dictate how a customer's demands can be met.

 もう1枚毛布を借りたいんですが……。
Mō ichi-mai mōfu o karitai n desu ga….

かしこまりました。これからお持ちします。
Kashikomarimashita. Korekara o-mochisimasu.

 隣の部屋がうるさいんですが……。
Tonari no heya ga urusai n desu ga….

申し訳ございません。別の部屋にお移りいただけますが、そうされますか。
Mōshiwake gozaimasen. Betsu no heya ni o-utsuri itadakemasu ga, sōsaremasu ka?

 部屋がタバコ臭いので、変えてもらえませんか。
Heya ga tabako kusai node, kaetemoraemasen ka?

別の部屋をご案内させていただきます。
Betsu no heya o go-annai sasete itadakimasu.

＊案内する：show, offer

 タクシーを呼んでもらいたいんですが……。
Takushī o yondemoraitai n desu ga…

かしこまりました。いつご出発でしょうか。
Kashikomarimashita. Itsu go-shuppatsu deshō ka?

＊出発する：leave (the hotel)

Unit 6

宿泊施設⑥
しゅくはくしせつ

Accommodations 6:
Other

Memorize other major requests that may come to the front desk.

CD-2 28

☐ 1　I can't get into my room...　　　▸ へや

☐ 2　I understand. I will go to your room with you. What is your room number?　　　▸ かしこまりました

☐ 3　Is there a simple map of the area?　　　▸ このへん
● the area →この辺、その辺
　　　　　　　へん　　へん

☐ 4　Here is a map of the area.　　　▸ しゅうへん

☐ 5　I think I'll be arriving at the hotel fairly late...　　　▸ ホテル
● fairly →かなり

☐ 6　That is not a problem. The front door is always open. About what time will you be arriving?　　　▸ だいじょうぶ

☐ 7　I'd like to extend my checkout time if possible...　　　▸ チェックアウト
● extend →延長する
　　　　　　えんちょう

☐ 8　Certainly. How long of an extension would you like?　　　▸ かしこまりました

第5章 宿泊施設

Meeting customer needs

Tips for Working in the Service Industry

While larger hotels have concierges, many hotels do not have such individuals. However, this means that front desk staff will need to perform these services, so prepare on a daily basis to handle such requests.

 部屋に入れなくなったんですが……。
Heya ni hairenakunatta n desu ga….

かしこまりました。では、お部屋までご一緒します。お部屋の番号は何番ですか。
Kashikomarimashita. Dewa, o-heya made go-issho shimasu. O-heya no bangō wa nan-ban desu ka?　　＊ご一緒する：the polite expression of "go with you"

 この辺の簡単な地図はありませんか。
Kono hen no kantanna chizu wa arimasen ka?　　＊簡単な：simple, rough

周辺のマップがございます。こちらです。
Shūhen no mappu ga gozaimasu. Kochira desu.

 ホテルに着くのがかなり遅くなりそうなのですが……。
Hoteru ni tsuku no ga kanari osokunarisō na no desu ga….

大丈夫です、玄関は開いておりますので。何時頃になりそうでしょうか。
Daijōbu desu, genkan wa aiteorimasu node. Nan-ji goro ni narisō deshō ka?

 チェックアウトの時間を延長したいのですが……。
Chekkuauto no jikan o enchō shitai no desu ga….

かしこまりました。延長のお時間はどうなさいますか。
Kashikomarimashita. Enchō no o-jikan wa dō nasaimasu ka?

Chapter 5 Accommodations

単語 & ミニフレーズ
Vocabulary + Mini-Phrases

宿泊施設 (しゅくはくしせつ)

日本語	ローマ字 / English
ツイン	*tsuin* / twin
ダブル	*daburu* / double
三人部屋 (さんにんべや)	*sanninbeya* / three-person room
和室 (わしつ)	*washitsu* / Japanese-style room
洋室 (ようしつ)	*yōshitsu* / Western-style room
ふとん	*futon* / futon
枕 (まくら)	*makura* / pillow
シーツ	*shītsu* / sheets
枕カバー (まくら)	*makurakabā* / pillowcase
浴衣 (ゆかた)	*yukata* / yukata
大浴場 (だいよくじょう)	*daiyokujō* / large public bath
オートロック	*ōtorokku* / auto-lock
カードキー	*kādokī* / card key
金庫 (きんこ)	*kinko* / safe
内線 (ないせん)	*naisen* / extension, internal line
インターネット	*intānetto* / Internet
ワイファイ環境 (かんきょう)	*waifai kankyō* / Wi-Fi environment
貸し出し (かしだし)	*kashidashi* / lend
(ヘヤー)ドライヤー	*(heyā) doraiyā* / hairdryer
アイロン	*airon* / iron
ロビー	*robī* / lobby
ラウンジ	*raunji* / lounge
プール	*pūru* / pool
サウナ	*sauna* / sauna
会議室 (かいぎしつ)	*kaigishitsu* / meeting room
宴会場 (えんかいじょう)	*enkaijō* / banquet room
非常口 (ひじょうぐち)	*hijōguchi* / emergency exit
非常階段 (ひじょうかいだん)	*hijōkaidan* / emergency stairs
両替 (りょうがえ)	*ryōgae* / money exchange
モーニングコール	*mōningukōru* / wake-up call
メモを預かって(あず)おります。	*Memo o azukatte orimasu.* / We have a memo for you.

第6章

その他のさまざまなサービス

Various Other Services

カラオケ店①〜②/
レンタルビデオ店①〜②/講座①〜③

Karaoke Stores 1-2 /
Rental Video Store 1-2 / Instructors 1-3

Unit 1

カラオケ店① (てん)
Karaoke Stores 1: Reception

Memorize basic expressions used at reception.

☐	1	Welcome. How many are in your party?	▸ いらっしゃいませ
☐	2	Do you have a membership card? • membership card → 会員証 (かいいんしょう)	▸ かいいんしょう
☐	3 (CUSTOMER)	How does the payment system here work?	▸ りょうきんシステム
☐	4	It is 500 yen an hour, and 300 yen for every 30 minute extension.	▸ いちじかん
☐	5	How long would you like to use the facilities?	▸ ごりようじかん
☐	6	"*Furītaimu*" is a better deal if you will be here for three or more hours. • a better deal → (お)得 (とく) *Free Time: The charge is the same no matter how long the facilities are used within a certain time period during one day.	▸ さんじかん
☐	7	Charges will change to our night rates after six, is that okay?	▸ ろくじから
☐	8 (CUSTOMER)	Is there a type of machine you would like to use?	▸ きしゅ

Various payment systems

Tips for Working in the Service Industry

There are various kinds of karaoke payment systems. "*Furītaimu*" may also depend on the store, whether it applies during that day's operating hours, during a specific time period (for example, 10 AM - 6 PM), or with no maximum time limit.

いらっしゃいませ。何名様ですか。
Irasshaimase. Nan-mē-sama desu ka?

会員証はお持ちですか。
Kaiinshō wa o-mochi desu ka?

料金システムはどのようになっていますか。
Ryōkin shisutemu wa donoyō ni natte imasu ka?

1時間500円で、延長の場合、30分ごとに300円追加されます。
Ichi-jikan gohyaku-en de, enchō no bāi, sanjuppun goto ni sanbyaku-en tsuika saremasu.

＊〜ごと(に)：every 〜

ご利用時間はいかがいたしますか。
Go-riyō jikan wa ikaga itashimasu ka?

3時間以上ですと、「フリータイム」のほうがお得です。
San-jikan ijō desuto, "furītaimu" no hō ga o-toku desu.

6時から夜料金になりますが、よろしいですか。
Roku-ji kara yoru ryōkin ni narimasu ga, yoroshī desu ka?

機種のご希望はございますか。
Kishu no go-kibō wa gozaimasu ka?

Unit 2

カラオケ店②
Karaoke 2: Explaining How to Use the Facilities

Memorize basic expressions regarding the use of services.

CD-2 / 30

☐ **1** Would you like to do a one-drink order or will you use the drink bar?
*One-drink order system: A single customer ordering a single drink.
*Drink bar: Customers can freely use the self-serve drink dispensers.
▶ ワンドリンク

☐ **2** We use a one-drink order system, so please make your orders using the phone in the room.
▶ ワンドリンクせい

☐ **3** Your room will be room number 305.
- room number 305 → 305号室(こうしつ)
▶ おへや

☐ **4** Please go up to the third floor using the elevator in the back there.
▶ あちら

☐ **5** (CUSTOMER) The remote control isn't working...
- remote control → リモコン
- not work → 効(き)かない
▶ リモコン

☐ **6** Please wait a moment. ...Please use this one.
▶ しょうしょう

☐ **7** Your time will be up in ten minutes. Would you like an extension?
▶ おじかん

☐ **8** We'd like a one hour extension, please. / No extension, please.
▶ いちじかん

第6章　その他のさまざまなサービス

"Wandorinku-sē"

Tips for Working in the Service Industry

A requirement for customers to order at least one drink per person. Many stores allow you to choose between this and a "*dorinkubā*" (Self-serve drink service).

ワンドリンクとドリンクバー、どちらになさいますか。
Wandorinku to dorinkubā, dochira ni nasaimasu ka?

ワンドリンク制となっておりますので、部屋からお電話でご注文ください。
Wandorinku sē to natte orimasu node, heya kara o-denwa de go-chūmon kudasai.

お部屋は305号室でございます。
O-heya ha sanbyakugo-gō shitsu de gozaimasu.

あちら奥のエレベーターで3階までお上がりください。
Achira oku no erebētā de san-gai made o-agari kudasai.

＊あちら奥の：in the back there

リモコンが効かないんですが……。
Rimokon ga kikanai n desu ga….

＊効く：work

少々お待ちください。・・・こちらをお使いください。
Shōshō o-machi kudasai. …..Kochira o o-tsukai kudasai.

お時間終了10分前ですが、延長はいかがなさいますか。
O-jikan shūryō juppun mae desu ga, enchō wa ikaga nasaimasu ka?

1時間延長でお願いします。／延長なしでお願いします。
Ichi-jikan enchō de onegai shimasu. / Enchō nashi de onegai shimasu.

Unit 3

レンタルビデオ店①

Rental Video Store 1:
Handling Customers on the Sales Floor / Card Procedures

Memorize expressions regarding how to help customers looking for a product or how to sign up for a card.

CD-2 31

☐ 1 *CUSTOMER* Where are the American TV drama series? ▸ アメリカ

☐ 2 This shelf. / All of the titles around here are also the same. ▸ こちら

☐ 3 *CUSTOMER* I'm looking for ABC's latest single... ▸ エービーシー
　　• latest → 最新(の)

☐ 4 I'm sorry, all of our copies are currently being rented. ▸ もうしわけございません
　　• being rented → 貸し出し中

☐ 5 Do you have an X card? ▸ エックスカード

☐ 6 We can make a card for you right away. Would you like to make one? ▸ カード

☐ 7 It is free to join, but there is a 300 yen yearly charge. ▸ にゅうかいきん
　　• yearly charge → 年会費

☐ 8 This card has expired. Would you like to renew it? ▸ こちら
　　• expire → 切れる

第6章 その他のさまざまなサービス

🍀 Methods of joining / renewing memberships

Tips for Working in the Service Industry

Joining or renewing a membership card may be somewhat annoying for customers. Be polite and efficient as you guide them through the process.

 アメリカのテレビドラマのシリーズはどこですか。
Amerika no terebidorama no sirīzu wa doko desu ka?

こちらの棚でございます。／この辺りが全部そうです。
Kochira no tana de gozaimasu. / Kono atari ga zenbu sō desu.

＊この辺り：around here

 ABCの最新シングルを探しているんですが…。
Ēbīshī no saishin shinguru o sagashiteiru n desu ga….

申し訳ございません。在庫はすべて貸し出し中でございます。
Mōshiwake gozaimasen. Zaiko wa subete kashidashi chū de gozaimasu.

Xカードはお持ちですか。
Ekkusu kādo wa o-mochi desu ka?

カードはすぐにお作りできますが、お作りになりますか。
Kādo wa suguni o-tsukuri dekimasu ga, o-tsukuri ni narimasu ka?

入会金は無料ですが、年会費として300円いただきます。
Nyūkaikin wa muryō desu ga, nenkaihi toshite sanbyaku-en itadakimasu.

 こちら、カードの有効期限が切れておりますが、更新されますか。
Kochira, kādo no yūkōkigen ga kirete orimasu ga, kōshin saremasu ka?

＊更新する：renew

Unit 4

レンタルビデオ店②
てん

Rental Video Store 2:
Confirming Use and Checkout

Memorize expressions relating to confirming rental periods and other specific use conditions, as well as relating to checkout.

CD-2
32

☐ 1 How many nights would you like to rent this video? ▸ ごりようはくすう

☐ 2   Three nights and four days. ▸ さんぱく

☐ 3 If you rent one more video, it will come out to a discounted total of 800 yen. ▸ もういっぽん

☐ 4 This is a new video and is not eligible for a discount. ▸ こちらは
   • new video → 新作
        しんさく

☐ 5 Three old titles for a use period of a week. That will come out to 600 yen total. ▸ きゅうさく
   *Generally titles that have been available for rent for a few months.

☐ 6 There will be a late fee of 400 yen for each video, for a total of 1200 yen. ▸ えんたいりょうきん
   • late fee → 延滞料金
        えんたいりょうきん

☐ 7 Excuse me, sir, there is no disc inside this [video case] … ▸ おきゃくさま

Frequently used counters

Tips for Working in the Service Industry

Be sure that you know the various kinds of counters used at rental video stores. Films use "*~hon*/ 本 "(when discussed as works, they may also use "*~saku*/ 作"), while CDs and DVDs use "*~mai*/ 枚", (when discussed as items or products, they may also use "*~ten*/ 点").

ご利用泊数はいかがなさいますか。
Go-ryō hakusū wa ikaga nasaimasu ka?

＊泊数は…か：How many nights …?

３泊４日で。
San-paku yokka de.

もう１本借りられると全部で800円になって、お得ですが……。
Mō ippon karirareruto zenbu de happyaku-en ni natte, o-toku desu ga….

こちらは新作ですので、割引の対象外になります。
Kochira wa shinsaku desu node, waribiki no taishōgai ni narimasu.

＊〜の対象外：not eligible for 〜

旧作３点、１週間のご利用で、合計600円になります。
Kyūsaku san-ten, isshūkan no go-ryō de, gōkē roppyaku-en ni narimasu.

延滞料金がそれぞれ400円かかりますので、合計で1200円いただきます。
Entai ryōkin ga sorezore yon'hyaku-en kakarimasu node, gōkē de sen nihyaku-en itadakimasu.

お客様、こちら、中身が入っておりませんが……。
O-kyaku-sama, kochira, nakami ga haitte orimasen ga….

Unit 5

講座①
Instructors 1: Language Instruction

Memorize basic expressions used during regular lessons.

- 1 Let us begin. ▸ では

- 2 Please open to page 25 of your textbook. ▸ きょうかしょ

- 3 Let's practice. ▸ れんしゅう
    - let's 〜 → 〜ましょう

- 4 Please repeat after me. ▸ わたしに

- 5 Please say that again. ▸ もういちど

- 6 That's good. ▸ いい…

- 7 That's all for today. ▸ では

- 8 Please review well for next time. ▸ よく

"*Hai.*" "*Dōzo.*"

Tips for Working in the Service Industry

When you want a student to repeat after you, first say "*Watashi ni tsuzuite itte kudasai.*"(Repeat after me), then after saying what needs to be repeated, indicate so by saying "*Hai.*" or "*Dōzo.*". It is also good to give a comment after they repeat the phrase such as "*Ī desu yo/motto ōkina koe de*" (Good / louder).

では、始めましょう。
Dewa, hajimemashō.

教科書の 25 ページを開いてください。
Kyōkasho no nijūgo-pēji o hiraite kudasai.

練習しましょう。
Renshū shimashō.

私に続いて言ってください。
Watashi ni tsuzuite itte kudasai.

＊私に続いて〜：〜 after me

もう一度言ってください。
Mō ichido itte kudasai.

いいですよ。
Ī desu yo.

では、今日はこれで終わります。
Dewa, kyō wa korede owarimasu.

よく復習しておいてください。
Yoku fukushū shite oite kudasai.

＊復習する：review ⇔ 予習する（prepare）

Unit 6

講座②
Instructors 2: Various Instruction

Memorize basic expressions used in many kinds of lectures such as cooking, music, sports, and more.

CD-2 34

☐ **1** I'm Tanaka, your instructor for today. Nice to meet you! ▸ ほんじつ

☐ **2** Are you ready? ▸ ようい

☐ **3** We'll start with me doing it first. Please watch carefully. ▸ では
• ~ carefully → 注意深く~する、よく~する

☐ **4** Like this. ▸ こんな

☐ **5** Did you understand? Now please try it yourself. ▸ わかりましたか

☐ **6** Let's do it together. ▸ いっしょに

☐ **7** Let's try that one more time. ▸ もういっかい

☐ **8** Please keep going. ▸ つづけて…

Not using a title for yourself

Tips for Working in the Service Industry

When introducing yourself during an initial class, do not call yourself "~*sensē*". For example, don't use a title and say something like, "*Nyūmon kurasu tantō no ~ desu.*" (I'm the teacher for the introductory class, ~.)

本日担当の田中です。よろしくお願いします。
Honjitsu tantō no Tanaka desu. Yoroshiku onegai shimasu.

＊担当(者)：person in charge

用意はいいですか。
Yōi wa ī desu ka?

では、まず私がやってみます。よく見ていてください。
Dewa, mazu watashi ga yattemimasu. Yoku mite ite kudasai.

こんな感じです。
Konna kanji desu.

わかりましたか。じゃ、ちょっとやってみてください。
Wakarimashita ka? Ja, chotto yatte mite kudasai.

一緒にやってみましょう。
Isshoni yattemimashō.

もう一回やってみましょう。
Mō ikkai yattemimashō.

続けてください。
Tsuzukete kudasai.

＊（～を）続ける：keep ～, keep ～ ing

Unit 7

講座③
Instructors 3: Various Instruction

Memorize basic expressions used in many kinds of lectures, such as cooking, music, sports, and more.

CD-2 35

☐	1	Good. Like that.	▶ いいですよ
☐	2	Very good.	▶ じょうず
☐	3	That's a little wrong. Like this.	▶ そこ
☐	4	You're putting a little too much force into it. / Please relax more. • use less force →力を抜く ⇔力を入れる	▶ ちょっと
☐	5	You're able to do it for the most part. • for the most part →大体、大部分は	▶ だいたい
☐	6	You're able to do it quite well now.	▶ だいぶ
☐	7	Let's start by reviewing what you learned last time.	▶ まず
☐	8	You'll be able to do it with practice. Don't worry.	▶ れんしゅう

Words of praise and encouragement

Tips for Working in the Service Industry

Use words of praise and encouragement as appropriate, such as "*Īdesu yo.*" (That's good), "*Īdesu ne.*" (Good), "*Yoku dekiteimasu.*" (You're doing a good job), "*Jōzudesu yo*"(Very good), "*Daibu jōtatsu shimashita ne.*" (You've gotten much better), and "*Renshū, ganbatte kudasai.*"(Work hard on your practice). This will encourage students.

いいですよ。そんな感じです。

Īdesu yo. Sonna kanji desu.

上手ですね。

Jōzu desu ne.

そこがちょっと違います。こうです。

Soko ga chotto chigaimasu. Kō desu.

＊こう：like this

ちょっと力が入っていますね。／もっと力を抜いてください。

Chotto chikara ga haitte imasu ne. / Motto chikara o nuite kudasai.

だいたいできています。

Daitai dekite imasu.

だいぶできるようになりましたね。

Daibu dekiru yō ni narimashita ne.

まず、前回の復習をしましょう。

Mazu, zenkai no fukushū o shimashō.

＊前回（／今回／次回）：last time(/this time/next time)

練習すればできます。大丈夫です。

Renshū sureba dekimasu. Daijōbu desu.

＊大丈夫：okay, fine

単語 & ミニフレーズ
Vocabulary + Mini-Phrases

その他のさまざまなサービス

新作	*shinsaku* new title
旧作	*kyūsaku* old title
キャンペーン	*kyanpēn* special promotion
身分証明書／身分証	*mibunshōmēsho/mibunshō* identification / ID
運転免許証	*untenmenkyoshō* driver's license
健康保険証／保険証	*kenkōhokenshō/hokenshō* health insurance card
本日、ご住所を確認できるものをお持ちでしょうか。	*Honjitsu, go-jūsho o kakunin dekiru mono o omochideshō ka.* Do you have anything we can use to confirm your address today?
ご返却ですね。確認させていただきますので、少々お待ちください。	*Go-henkyaku desune. Kakunin sasete itadakimasunode, shōshō omachikudasai.* You're returning this? Please wait a moment as I confirm.
講師／インストラクター	*kōshi/insutorakutā* lecturer/instructor
初心者／初めての方	*shoshinsha/hajimete no kata* beginner
手本	*tehon* model
上達する	*jōtatsusuru* to improve
基本が大切です。	*Kihon ga taisetsu desu.* The basics are important.
センスがありますよ。	*Sensu ga arimasu yo.* You have a sense for this.
その調子で続けてください。	*Sono chōshi de tsuzukete kudasai.* Please continue like that.

第7章
だいしょう

電話基本会話
でんわきほんかいわ
Basic Telephone Conversations

電話応対①〜⑤
でんわおうたい

Answering the Phone 1-5

Unit 1

電話応対①
Answering the Phone 1: Taking Reservations at a Restaurant

Memorize basic expressions used when taking reservations at a restaurant, such as confirming the date, time, and party size.

CD-2 36

☐ 1	Yes, this is the restaurant Fuji.	▶ はい
☐ 2 (CUSTOMER)	I'd like to make a reservation.	▶ よやく
☐ 3	Certainly. For what day would you like to make a reservation?	▶ かしこまりました
☐ 4	For what time would you like your reservation? / When would you like your reservation to be?	▶ おじかん
☐ 5 (CUSTOMER)	I was hoping for seven tonight...	▶ きょうの
☐ 6	How many are in your party?	▶ なんめい…
☐ 7	May I ask for your name?	▶ おなまえ
☐ 8	Then I'll make your reservation for tonight at seven, party of three.	▶ ではほんじつ

🍀 Don't slack, even when people aren't looking at you

Tips for Working in the Service Industry

Saying straightforward things such as "*Dare desu ka?*" (Who is this?) and "*Namae wa nan desu ka?*" (What is your name?) will give off a rude impression. Use polite expressions instead such as "Dochira sama deshō ka?" and "O-namae o itadakemasu ka?" Also, when on the telephone, even though the person you are talking to cannot see you, you should not relax your attention. Speak politely with a bright smile on your face, and hang up the phone quietly as well.

はい、レストラン「ふじ」です。

Hai, resutoran "Fuji" desu.

予約をお願いします。

Yoyaku o onegai shimasu.

かしこまりました。お日にちはいつがご希望でしょうか。

Kashikomarimashita. O-hinichi wa itsu ga go-kibō deshō ka?

お時間はいかがでしょうか。／お時間はいつがよろしいでしょうか。

O-jikan wa ikaga deshō ka? / O-jikan wa itsu ga yoroshī deshō ka?

今日の夜 7 時にお願いしたいんですが……。

Kyō no yoru shichi-ji ni onegai shitai n desu ga….

何名様でしょうか。

Nan-mē-sama deshō ka?

お名前をいただけますか。

O-namae o itadakemasu ka?

では本日午後 7 時、3 名様でご予約を承りました。

Dewa honjitsu gogo shichi-ji, san-mē-sama de go-yoyaku o uketamawarimashita.

Unit 2

電話応対②
Answering the Phone 2: Taking Reservations at a Hotel

Memorize expressions relating to reserving rooms at a hotel.

☐ **1** Thank you for calling. This is Sakura Hotel. ▶ おでんわ

☐ **2** [CUSTOMER] I'd like to make a reservation... ▶ よやく

☐ **3** May I ask when you will be checking in? ▶ おひにち

☐ **4** How many nights will you be staying with us? ▶ なんぱく
　　・〈About hotel〉 How many nights ... ? → 何泊…か

☐ **5** May I ask what room type you would like? ▶ おへや

☐ **6** I'm sorry, we don't have any reservations available on the 15th. The 16th is open, however... ▶ もうしわけございません
　　・open → 空いている、空きがある

☐ **7** This room type is 8,000 yen a night, including tax. ▶ こちらの
　　・〜 yen a night → 1泊〜円　　・including tax → 税込みで

☐ **8** Then I'll reserve you a single room for the two nights of July 16 and 17. ▶ ではしちがつ…

Being accurate when taking reservations

Tips for Working in the Service Industry

When taking reservations, confirm with the customer so that you get the date, number of individuals, room type, and so on correctly.

お電話ありがとうございます。さくらホテルです。
O-denwa arigatōgozaimasu. Sakura Hoteru desu.

 予約をお願いしたいんですが……。
Yoyaku o onegai shitai n desu ga….

お日にちはいつからをご希望でしょうか。
O-hinichi wa itsu kara o go-kibō deshō ka?

＊日にち：date

何泊のご利用でしょうか。
Nan-paku no go-riyō deshō ka?

お部屋のタイプはいかがなさいますか。
O-heya no taipu wa ikaga nasaimasu ka?

申し訳ございません。15日は予約でいっぱいです。16日でしたら空いておりますが……。
Mōshiwake gozaimasen. Jūgo-nichi wa yoyaku de ippai desu. Jūroku-nichi deshitara aite orimasu ga...

＊（予約で）いっぱい：no vacancy, full occupancy

こちらのタイプですと、税込みで、ご1泊8000円になります。
Kochira no taipu desu to, zēkomi de, go-ippaku hassen-en ni narimasu.

では7月16日と17日、シングルの2泊でご予約を承りました。
Dewa shichi-gatsu jūroku-nichi to jūshichi-nichi, shinguru no ni-haku de go-yoyaku o uketamawarimashita.

Unit 3

電話応対 ③
Answering the Phone 3: When Someone is Not Present

Memorize expressions used when someone asked for is not present.

CD-2 38

☐ 1 **CUSTOMER** My name is Mori of ABC. Is store manager Tanaka there?
• store manager →店長
▶ エービーシーの…

☐ 2 Tanaka has not arrived yet. Shall I have him call you back later?
• call someone back →折り返し電話する
▶ たなかは

☐ 3 Tanaka is currently out for lunch... Shall I tell him to call you when he returns?
▶ たなかは

☐ 4 Shall I have him call you back?
▶ こちらから

☐ 5 **CUSTOMER** Could you have him call me back when he returns?
▶ おもどりに

☐ 6 Tanaka is currently out of the office, is it an urgent matter?
• be out →外出している、出かけている
▶ たなかは

☐ 7 Tanaka is out, but he is supposed to return at 3:00.
▶ たなかは

☐ 8 Then I will try contacting him on his cell phone.
▶ では

"*Uchi*" and "*Soto*"

Tips for Working in the Service Industry

There is a way of thinking in Japanese of "*Uchi*" (inside, in-group) and "*Soto*" (outside group). When speaking to customers, other store staff are considered individuals who are a part of "*Uchi*", and so respectful language is not used with them. For example, the phrase "*Nochihodo tōten tenchō no Tanaka ga o-ukagai shimasu.*" (Tanaka, the store's manager, will be here shortly) should be used.

ABCの森と申しますが、田中店長はいらっしゃいますか。
Ēbīshī no Mori to mōshimasu ga, Tanaka tenchō wa irasshaimasu ka?

田中はまだ出社しておりません。折り返しお電話差し上げるようにいたしましょうか。
Tanaka wa mada shussha shite orimasen. Orikaeshi o-denwa sashiageru yō ni itashimashō ka?　＊差し上げる: the polite expression of "あげる（give）"

田中は今、お昼に出ておりますが……。戻りましたら、お電話するように申し伝えましょうか。
Tanaka wa ima, o-hiru ni dete orimasu ga…. Modorimashitara, o-denwa suru yō ni mōshitutaemashō ka?
　　＊(お)昼: lunch　＊申し伝える: the polite expression of "tell"

こちらからお電話させましょうか。
Kochira kara o-denwa sasemashō ka?

お戻りになったら、コールバックをいただけますか。
O-modori ni nattara, kōrubakku o itadakemasu ka?

田中はただ今外出しておりますが、お急ぎでしょうか。
Tanaka wa tadaima gaishutsu shite orimasu ga, o-isogi deshō ka?

田中は出かけておりまして、戻りが3時の予定です。
Tanaka wa dekakete orimashite, modori ga san-ji no yotē desu.

では、携帯に連絡をとってみます。
Dewa, kētai ni renraku o tottemimasu.　＊携帯: the abbreviation of "cell phone"

Unit 4

電話応対④
Answering the Phone 4: Messages

Memorize basic expressions relating to messages.

CD-2 39

☐ 1	 **Can I ask you to take a message?** • take a message →伝言を預かる	▶ でんごん
☐ 2	**Yes, please go ahead.**	▶ かしこまりました
☐ 3	**So you'd like to change the time you'd agreed on. I understand.** • agree on 〜 →〜を約束する	▶ おやくそく
☐ 4	**(I'm sorry.) Could you please repeat your name one more time?**	▶ もういちど
☐ 5	**Then I will let her know.**	▶ では
☐ 6	**My name is Tanaka, and I have taken your message.**	▶ わたくし
☐ 7	**Would you like me to take a message?**	▶ ごでんごん
☐ 8	**I can take a message if you'd like...** • if you'd like →よろしければ	▶ よろしければ

第7章 電話基本会話

Don't make customers wait

Tips for Working in the Service Industry

It is important to not make customers wait unnecessarily on the phone. Perhaps they are very busy people for whom calling is difficult. Also, be aware that some customers may have to pay a fee when calling you.

 伝言をお願いできますか。
Dengon o onegai dekimasu ka?

かしこまりました。では、どうぞ。
Kashikomarimashita. Dewa, dōzo.

お約束の時間を変更されたいとのことですね。承知いたしました。
O-yakusoku no jikan o henkō saretai to no koto desu ne? Shōchi itashimashita.
＊承知いたしました：the polite expression of "わかりました"

（恐れ入ります。）もう一度お名前をいただけますか。
(Osoreirimasu.) Mō ichido o-namae o itadakemasu ka?

では、伝えておきます。
Dewa, tsutaete okimasu.

わたくし、田中が承りました。
Watakushi, Tanaka ga uketamawarimashita.
＊（伝言を）承る：take a message

ご伝言を承りましょうか。
Go-dengon o uketamawarimashō ka?

よろしければ、ご伝言を承りますが……。
Yoroshikereba, go-dengon o uketamawarimasu ga….

Chapter 7　Basic Telephone Conversations

Unit 5

電話応対⑤
Answering the Phone 5: Other

Memorize expressions used when transferring people or putting them on hold.

☐ 1　What is the nature of your call? / May I ask what you're calling about?　▸ どういった…

☐ 2　I will transfer you to the person in charge; please wait a moment.　▸ たんとうしゃ
　　● transfer → つなぐ

☐ 3　〈After being transferred on the phone〉
　　Hello, your call has been transferred. My name is Tanaka, and I am in charge.　▸ おでんわ

☐ 4　I will look it up for you. Please wait a moment. …Thank you for waiting.　▸ おしらべ…

☐ 5　It's a little hard to hear you…　▸ ちょっと

☐ 6　I'm sorry, could you please repeat that?　▸ すみません

☐ 7　Shall I set it aside for you?　▸ おとりおき
　　● set ～ aside → ～をお取り置きする

☐ 8　I'm sorry, may I ask who's calling?　▸ しつれい

第7章 電話基本会話

 Stay cool and don't become emotional

Tips for Working in the Service Industry

There are many kinds of people who are customers. For example, some may complain that your Japanese is hard to understand. Even then, give a sincere apology and repeat yourself, dealing with the customer in a pleasant way.

どういったことでしょうか。／どういったご用件でしょうか。
Dōitta koto deshō ka? / Dōitta go-yōken deshō ka?

＊どういった：どういう〜、どんな〜（what kind of 〜）　　＊用件：affair, business

担当者におつなぎしますので、しばらくお待ちください。
Tantōsha ni o-tsunagi shimasu node, shibaraku o-machi kudasai.

〈電話を取り次がれて〉お電話代わりました。担当の田中と申します。
〈*Denwa o toritsugarete*〉 *O-denwa kawarimashita. Tantō no Tanaka to mōshimasu.*

お調べしますので、少々お待ちください。・・・お待たせしました。
O-shirabe shimasu node, shōshō o-machi kudasai. ....O-matase shimashita.

ちょっとお電話が遠いようなんですが……。
Chotto o-denwa ga tōi yō na n desu ga....　　＊（電話が）遠い：hard to hear

---

すみません、もう一度よろしいですか。
Sumimasen, mō ichido yoroshī desu ka?

お取り置きしましょうか。
O-torioki shimashō ka?

失礼ですが、どちら様でしょうか。
Shitsurē desu ga, dochira-sama deshō ka?

Chapter 7 Basic Telephone Conversations

203

単語 & ミニフレーズ
Vocabulary + Mini-Phrases

あいにく、田中は本日は休ませていただいております。	Ainiku, Tanaka wa honjitsu wa yasumasete itadaite orimasu. Unfortunately, Tanaka is taking the day off.
田中は本日はもう失礼させていただきました。	Tanaka wa honjitsu wa mō shitsurē sasete itadakimashita. Tanaka has already left for the day.
青木はただ今ほかの電話に出ております。	Aoki wa tadaima hoka no denwa ni dete orimasu. Aoki is currently on another phone call.
念のため、お電話番号をお願いいたします。	Nen no tame, o-denwabangō o onegai itashimasu. May I have your phone number, just to be sure?
恐れ入りますが、もう一度、御社名とお名前をお伺いしてもよろしいでしょうか。	Osoreirimasuga, mō ichido, on-shamē to o-namae o o-ukagai shite mo yoroshī deshō ka? I'm sorry, but may I ask you for your company name and your name one more time?
下のお名前もお伺いしてよろしいでしょうか。	Shita no o-namae mo o-ukagai shite yoroshī deshō ka? May I ask for your given name as well?
恐れ入りますが、どのような字をお書きになりますか。	Osoreirimasuga, donoyōna ji o o-kaki ni narimasu ka? I'm sorry, but what characters do you use to write that name?
一度切らせていただきます。	Ichi-do kirasete itadakimasu. Allow me to hang up once.

第8章
緊急・トラブル
Emergencies / Trouble

急病人①〜②／地震／火災／
避難／落とし物・忘れ物

Emergency Cases1-2 ／ Earthquakes ／ Fires ／
Evacuating ／ Dropped and Forgotten Items

Unit 1

急病人 ①
きゅうびょうにん

Emergency Cases 1: Speaking to Individuals

Memorize expressions often used when first speaking to someone who is having a medical emergency, such as phrases for confirming their condition.

CD-2 41

☐ **1** Is something the matter? ▸ どう

☐ **2** Are you all right? Can you hear me? ▸ だいじょうぶ

☐ **3** [CUSTOMER] I don't feel very well... ▸ ちょっと

☐ **4** [CUSTOMER] I was feeling a little dizzy. ▸ ちょっと
- dizzy →めまいがする

☐ **5** Does it hurt anywhere? ▸ どこか

☐ **6** Please rest here for a bit. ▸ しばらく

☐ **7** Please make yourself as comfortable as possible. ▸ なるべく
- relieve yourself →楽にする
  らく

☐ **8** Would you like to lie down? ▸ ちょっと
- lie down →横になる、寝る
  よこ　　　　　ね

Start with first aid

Tips for Working in the Service Industry

If someone is having a medical emergency, conduct first aid by speaking to them, having them lie down, stopping bleeding, and so on. Then check to make sure they are okay and work with those accompanying them or family members to move on to the next steps, such as calling an ambulance.

どうなさいましたか。
Dō nasaimashita ka?

大丈夫ですか、聞こえますか。
Daijōbu desu ka? Kikoemasu ka?

ちょっと気分が悪くて……。
Chotto kibun ga warukute….

＊気分が悪い：feel ill

ちょっとめまいがしたんです。
Chotto memai ga shita n desu.

どこか痛いところがありますか。
Dokoka itai tokoro ga arimasu ka?

しばらくこちらで休んでください。
Shibaraku kochira de yasunde kudasai.

なるべく楽にしてください。
Narubeku raku ni shite kudasai.

＊なるべく〜：as 〜 as possible

ちょっと横になりますか。
Chotto yoko ni narimasu ka?

Unit 2

急病人 ②
きゅうびょうにん

**Emergency Cases 2:
Confirmation**

Memorize expressions used to confirm the wishes or condition of someone having a medical emergency.

CD-2 42

⟨A nearby person⟩

☐ **1** He suddenly collapsed. ▸ きゅうに
   ● collapse → 倒れる
   　　　　　　　たお

☐ **2** Should I call an ambulance? ▸ きゅうきゅうしゃ

☐ **3** I'll call an ambulance right away. ▸ いますぐ
   ● right away → 今すぐ、すぐに
   　　　　　　　 いま

☐ **4** Can you walk? ▸ あるけ…

☐ **5** Is anyone with you? ▸ どたなか

☐ **6** Are you alone today? ▸ きょうは

☐ **7** Are you a family member? / Are you an acquaintance? ▸ ごかぞく
   ● acquaintance →（知り合い→）お知り合いの方
   　　　　　　　　　 し　あ　　　　　し　あ　　かた

☐ **8** Could you please tell me the phone number of a family member? ▸ ごかぞく

第8章 緊急・トラブル

A quick response is most important

Tips for Working in the Service Industry

Speed is highly important in an emergency, so work to use easy to understand and simple expressions. There is no need to become nervous and over think your words.

〈近くにいる別の人〉 急に倒れたんです。
〈chikaku ni iru betsu no hito〉 Kyū ni taoreta n desu.

救急車をお呼びしましょうか。
Kyūkyūsha o o-yobi shimashō ka?

今すぐ救急車をお呼びします。
Imasugu kyūkyūsha o o-yobi shimasu.

＊今すぐ：right away

歩けますか。
Arukemasu ka?

どなたかお連れの方はいますか。
Donataka o-tsure no kata wa imasu ka?

＊お連れの方（＝連れの人）：your companion

今日はお一人ですか。
Kyō wa o-hitori desu ka?

ご家族の方ですか。／お知り合いの方ですか。
Go-kazoku no kata desu ka? / O-shiriai no kata desu ka?

ご家族のお電話番号を教えていただけますか。
Go-kazoku no o-denwa bangō o oshiete itadakemasu ka?

Chapter 8 Emergencies／Trouble

209

Unit 3

地震
じしん
Earthquakes:
Basic Responses When an Earthquake Strikes

Memorize initial phrases to use to make sure customers are safe when an earthquake strikes.

CD-2 43

☐ 1 Please stay down low. ▸ しせい

☐ 2 Please protect your head. ▸ あたま

☐ 3 Please take cover under a table or another object. ▸ つくえ

☐ 4 Please stay away from window glass. ▸ まどガラス
- stay away from 〜→〜から離れる
  はな

☐ 5 Please be careful for items that may collapse or fall from overhead. ▸ うえから

☐ 6 Please be careful of falling objects. ▸ らっかぶつ
- falling objects →落下物
  らっ か ぶつ

☐ 7 Please ensure your safety where you are until the shaking has subsided. ▸ ゆれ

第8章 緊急・トラブル

In the case of an earthquake...

Tips for Working in the Service Industry

Learn the basics of disaster prevention. In the case of an earthquake, this means protecting your head, being careful of objects that may fall, getting away from glass objects, staying still in a safe location until the strong shaking has stopped, and extinguishing fires.

姿勢を低くしてください。
Shisē o hikuku shite kudasai.

＊姿勢：position, posture

頭を守ってください。
Atama o mamotte kudasai.

机の下に身を隠すなどしてください。
Tsukue no shita ni mi o kakusu nado shite kudasai.

＊身：one's body, oneself

窓ガラスから離れてください。
Madogarasu kara hanarete kudasai.

上から落ちてくるものや倒れてくるものに気をつけてください。
Ue kara ochitekuru mono ya taoretekuru mono ni ki o tsukete kudasai.

落下物に気をつけてください。
Rakkabutsu ni ki o tsukete kudasai.

揺れが収まるまで、その場で安全を確保してください。
Yure ga osamaru made, sonoba de anzen o kakuho shite kudasai.

＊確保する：secure, ensure

Unit 4

火災(かさい)
Fires:
Basic Responses Regarding Fires

Memorize instructive and guiding phrases used when a fire occurs or when a fire may occur.

☐ 1 　The emergency alarm has been sounded, we are currently confirming the safety situation. ▶ さきほど
　　• emergency alarm →非常(ひじょう)ベル

☐ 2 　Please stay where you are for now. ▶ このまま

☐ 3 　The fire alarm has been sounded, but there was no outbreak of fire. ▶ さきほど
　　• fire alarm →火災報知器(かさいほうちき)

☐ 4 　A small fire had occurred in the building earlier, but it has been safely put out. ▶ さきほど
　　• small fire →ボヤ
　　• be put out [about fire] →（火が）収(おさ)まる、（火が）消(け)される

☐ 5 　A fire has occurred; please promptly evacuate. ▶ かさい

☐ 6 　Please place a wet handkerchief over your nose and mouth and avoid inhaling smoke. ▶ ぬれた

第8章 緊急・トラブル

 Regular checks are important

Tips for Working in the Service Industry

It is important to know escape methods and routes in advance. Make sure that you will not become panicked in the case that you have to guide customers.

先ほど非常ベルが鳴りましたので、安全確認をしております。

Sakihodo hijō-beru ga narimashita node, anzenkakunin o shite orimasu.

このままでしばらくお待ちください。

Konomama de shibaraku o-machi kudasai.

先ほど火災報知器が鳴りましたが、火災の発生はありませんでした。

Sakihodo kasai-hōchiki ga narimashitaga, kasai no hassē wa arimasen deshita.

＊発生する：occur

先ほどビル内でボヤが発生しましたが、火は収まり、安全が確認されました。

Sakihodo biru nai de boya ga hassē shimashita ga, hi wa osamari, anzen ga kakunin saremashita.

火災が発生しておりますので、速やかに避難してください。

Kasai ga hassē shite orimasu node, sumiyakani hinan shite kudasai.

＊速やかに：promptly

濡れたハンカチで鼻と口を押さえて、煙を吸わないようにしてください。

Nureta hankachi de hana to kuchi o osaete, kemuri o suwanai yō ni shite kudasai.

Chapter 8 / Emergencies / Trouble

213

Unit 5

避難(ひなん)
Evacuating: Evacuating Safely

Memorize instructive and guiding phrases used to safely evacuate people when a disaster strikes.

☐ 1	Please act calmly.	▶ おちついて
☐ 2	Please cooperate in following staff instructions.	▶ スタッフ
☐ 3	Please do not use the elevators.	▶ エレベーター
☐ 4	Please evacuate using the emergency stairs. • emergenct stairs → 非常階段(ひじょうかいだん)	▶ ひじょうかいだん
☐ 5	The emergency exit is at the end of this hallway. • emergency exit → 非常口(ひじょうぐち) • the end of 〜 → 〜の突(つ)き当(あ)たり	▶ ひじょうぐち6
☐ 6	Please evacuate without panicking or shoving.	▶ あわてず
☐ 7	Please follow us.	▶ わたしども

第8章 緊急・トラブル

Conveying precise and correct information

Tips for Working in the Service Industry

When evacuating, information about locations and routes becomes very important. It is key to use easy to understand and simple sentences to convey correct information.

落ち着いて行動してください。
Ochitsuite kōdō shite kudasai.

スタッフの指示に従うよう、ご協力ください。
Sutaffu no shiji ni shitagau yō, go-kyōryoku kudasai.

*スタッフ：staff

エレベーターは使わないでください。
Erebētā wa tsukawanaide kudasai.

非常階段を使って避難してください。
Hijōkaidan o tsukatte hinan shite kudasai.

非常口はこの廊下の突き当たりです。
Hijōguchi wa kono rōka no tsukiatari desu.

*突き当たり：end

慌てず、押し合わずに避難してください。
Awatezu, oshiawazu ni hinan shite kudasai.

*〜し合う：〜 each other

私どもの後についてきてください。
Watakushidomo no ato ni tsuite kite kudasai.

Unit 6 落とし物・忘れ物
Lost and Forgotten Items

Memorize expressions relating to cases such as when customers lose their wallets or forget their belongings.

CD-2 46

☐ **1** Excuse me, I was over there this morning. Did you find a lost wallet? ▶ すみません
  • dropped wallet → さいふの落とし物

☐ **2** What area were you sitting in? ▶ どのあたり

☐ **3** Allow me to check; please wait a moment. ▶ かくにんします

☐ **4** I checked, sir, but there was no such item. ▶ おきゃくさま
  • such item → そのようなもの、それらしいもの

☐ **5** We have not received any such lost items at this point. ▶ いまのところ
  • at this point → 今のところ

☐ **6** Um, I believe I forgot my umbrella at your store. Could you please look for it for me? ▶ あのう

☐ **7** What kind of umbrella is it? ▶ どんな

☐ **8** We found it, ma'am. We will hold on to it here, so please come back to the store. ▶ おきゃくさま

Don't just say "*Nai*"

Tips for Working in the Service Industry

These are major issues for people asking questions. Instead of simply saying that there is no such thing, be sure to check once again and properly address their concerns.

 すみません、今朝そちらに行ったんですが、財布の落とし物はなかったでしょうか。
Sumimasen, kesa sochira ni itta n desu ga, saifu no otoshimono wa nakatta deshō ka?

どの辺りにお座りになりましたか。
Dono atari ni o-suwari ni narimashita ka?

確認しますので、少々お待ちください。
Kakunin shimasu node, shōshō o-machi kudasai.
＊確認する：check

お客様、確認しましたが、それらしいものはございませんでした。
O-kyaku-sama, kakunin shimashita ga, sorerashī mono wa gozaimasen deshita.

今のところ、そのような落とし物は届いておりません。
Imanotokoro, sonoyōna otoshimono wa todoite orimasen.

あのう、お店に傘を置き忘れたみたいなんですが、見てもらえますか。
Anō, o-mise ni kasa o okiwasureta mitai na n desu ga, mite moraemasu ka?

どんな傘でしょうか。
Donna kasa deshō ka?

お客様、ございました。では、こちらで保管しておきますので、また、お店のほうにお越しください。
O-kyaku-sama, gozaimashita. Dewa, kochira de hokan shiteokimasu node, mata, o-mise no hō ni okoshi kudasai.
＊〜を保管する：keep 〜 safe, hold on to 〜

単語 & ミニフレーズ
Vocabulary + Mini-Phrases

緊急・トラブル

日本語	ローマ字 / English
貧血 (ひんけつ)	*hinketsu* — anemia
めまい	*memai* — dizziness
吐き気 (はけ)	*hakike* — nausea
腹痛 (ふくつう)	*fukutsū* — stomachache
気を失う (きうしな)	*ki o ushinau* — lose consciousness
血が出る／出血する (ちでる／しゅっけつ)	*chi ga deru / shukketsusuru* — bleed / to bleed
震えています。(ふる)	*Furueteimasu.* — I am shaking.
意識はあります。(いしき)	*Ishiki wa arimasu.* — He is conscious.
出血しています。(しゅっけつ)	*Shukketsushiteimasu.* — I am bleeding.
無理しないでください。(むり)	*Murishinaide kudasai.* — Please don't force yourself.
壁にぶつかる (かべ)	*kabe ni butsukaru* — run into a wall
けがをする	*kega o suru* — sustain an injury
安全(な) (あんぜん)	*anzen(na)* — safe
震度 (しんど)	*shindo* — seismic intensity
津波 (つなみ)	*tsunami* — tsunami
余震 (よしん)	*yoshin* — aftershock
揺れる (ゆ)	*yureru* — shake
消火器 (しょうかき)	*shōkaki* — fire extinguisher
危ないから近づかないでください。(あぶ / ちか)	*Abunai kara chikazukanaide kudasai.* — Please do not go close, it is dangerous.
慌てないでください。(あわ)	*Awatenaide kudasai.* — Please do not panic.

丁寧表現早見表
Polite Language Reference Sheet

1. 尊敬語 / Respectful Language

表現例 / Example Expression

		表現例
いる (To be)	いらっしゃる	●今、どちらにいらっしゃいますか。
行く (To go)	いらっしゃる、行かれる	●昨日はどちらにいらっしゃいましたか。 ●美術館へはもう行かれましたか。
来る (To come)	いらっしゃる、おいでになる、見える、お越しになる	●何時にいらっしゃいますか。 ●タクシーでおいでになりますか。 ●田中様がお見えになりました。 ●いつお越しになりますか。
する (To do)	なさる、される	●コピーをなさいますか。 ●チャージをされますか。
食べる (To eat)	召し上がる	●デザートを召し上がりますか。
飲む (To drink)	召し上がる、お飲みになる	●どうぞ、一杯召し上がってください。 ●何をお飲みになりますか。
言う (To say)	おっしゃる	●もう一度おっしゃってください。
見る (To see)	ご覧になる	●メニューをご覧になりますか。 ●あちらをご覧ください。
聞く (To hear)	お聞きになる	●場所はお聞きになりましたか。
尋ねる (To ask)	お尋ねになる	●受付でお尋ねください。
知る (To learn)	お知りになる	●詳しくお知りになりたい場合は、こちらにお電話ください。
知っている (To know)	ご存じ	●よくご存じですね。
わかる (To understand)	おわかりになる、ご理解いただく	●場所はおわかりになりますか。 ●ご理解いただけますか。 ●どうぞ、ご理解ください。
会う (To meet)	お会いになる、会われる	●ご家族とお会いになれましたか。
帰る (To return)	お帰りになる、帰られる	●田中様はもうお帰りになりました。 ●こちらの出口からお帰りください。
待つ (To wait)	お待ちになる、お待ちくださる	●お待ちになりますか。 ●少しお待ちくだされば、大丈夫です。
座る (To sit)	おかけになる、お座りになる	●こちらにおかけになってお待ちください。
着る (To wear)	お召しになる、召す	●一度お召しになってみてください。
持つ (To have)	お持ちでいらっしゃる	●かさはお持ちでいらっしゃいますか。

動詞	尊敬語	例文
持っていく To take with	お持ちになる	・かさをお持ちになってください。
持ってくる To bring	お持ちになる	・チケットをお持ちになってください。
連れる To take with	お連れになる	・お連れのお客様がお待ちです。
出発する To depart	お発ちになる	・何時に東京をお発ちになりますか。
着く To arrive	お着きになる	・何時に東京にお着きになりますか。
与える To give	くださる	・ご予約をくださり、ありがとうございます。
もらう To receive	お受け取りになる	・チケットはお受け取りになりましたか。
返す To return	お戻しになる、お返しになる	・カギはこちらにお戻しください。
買う To buy	お求めになる、お買い求めになる、お買い上げになる	・お求めの商品はこちらでしょうか。 ・売店でお買い求めになれます。 ・お買い上げ、ありがとうございます。
話す To speak	お話しになる、話される	・日本語を話されますか。
読む To read	お読みになる	・後でよくお読みになっておいてください。
乗る To ride	ご乗車になる、ご乗車される	・バスにご乗車になってお待ちください。
急ぐ To hurry	お急ぎになる、急がれる	・お急ぎになったほうがいいと思います。
ゆっくりする To be at ease	ごゆっくりなさる、ごゆっくりされる	・どうぞ、ごゆっくりなさってください。
出かける To leave	お出かけになる、出かけられる	・何時にお出かけになりますか。
電話に出る To pick up the phone	電話にお出になる	・電話にお出になりませんでした。
気に入る To have an interest in	お気に召す	・お気に召しましたか。
声をかける To call out to	声をおかけになる、お声がけになる	・いつでもお声がけください。
やめる To stop	おやめになる	・こちらの赤はおやめになりますか。
間違える To mistake	お間違えになる	・席をお間違えにならないようにしてください。
けがをする To injure oneself	けがをされる	・けがをされないよう、ご注意ください。
利用する To use	ご利用になる、利用される	・袋はご利用になりますか。 ・こちらを利用されるのは初めてですか。
注文する To order	ご注文になる、注文される	・いつ、ご注文になりましたか。 ・もう注文されましたか。
キャンセルする To cancel	キャンセルなさる	・キャンセルなさいますか。

2. 謙譲語／Humble Language

表現例／Example Expression

いる To be	おる	●午後はずっと店におります。
行く To go	うかがう、参る	●これからお部屋に伺います。
来る To come	参る	●明日、2時ごろに参ります。
する To do	させていただく	●では、お会計をさせていただきます。
言う To say	申す、申し上げる	●では、番号を申し上げます。
見る To see	拝見する	●チケットを拝見します
聞く To hear	うかがう、お伺いする、お聞きする、拝聴する	●お名前をうかがっても、よろしいですか。
尋ねる To ask	お伺いする、お尋ねする、お聞きする	●ご注文をお伺いします。
知る To learn	存じる、存じ上げる、承知する	●お名前は存じております。
知らない To not know	存じてない、存じ上げない	●詳しくは存じ上げません。
わかる To understand	かしこまる、承知する	●ご予約、かしこまりました。
会う To meet	お目にかかる	●お目にかかったことがございます。
帰る To return	失礼する、帰らせていただく	●田中は本日はもう失礼いたしました。
待つ To wait	お待ちする	●では、ご連絡をお待ちしております。
座る To sit	座らせていだく	●では、座らせていただきます。
あげる To give	差し上げる	●こちらの袋は差し上げます。 ●また、ご連絡を差し上げます。
もらう To receive	いただく、頂戴する	●お申し込みをいただき、ありがとうございます。
見せる To show	ご覧に入れる、お見せする	●サンプルをご覧に入れます。
持っていく To bring	お持ちする	●メニューをお持ちします。
預かる To hold onto	お預かりする	●カードをお預かりします。
返す To return	お返しする	●カードをお返しします。
調べる To investigate	お調べする	●お調べしますので、少々お待ちください。
知らせる To inform	お知らせする	●メールでお知らせします。

付ける(つける) To include	お付けする(つけ)	●おはしはお付けしますか。
下げる(さげる) To take away	お下げする(さ)	●メニューをお下げします。
電話する(でんわ) To phone	お電話する(でんわ)	●後でまた、お電話します。
説明する(せつめい) To explain	ご説明する(せつめい)	●では、ご説明いたします。
案内する(あんない) To guide	ご案内する(あんない)	●席をご案内いたします。

3. さまざまな丁寧表現(ていねいひょうげん) / Various Polite Expressions

明日(あした) Tomorrow	明日(あす)	去年(きょねん) Last year	昨年(さくねん)	どこ Where	どちら
明後日(あさって) The day after tomorrow	明後日(みょうごにち)	一昨年(おととし) Two years ago	一昨年(いっさくねん)	こっち Here	こちら
昨日(きのう) Yesterday	昨日(さくじつ)	もうすぐ Soon	間もなく(ま)	あっち Over there	あちら
一昨日(おととい) The day before yesterday	一昨日(いっさくじつ)	いま Now	ただいま	そっち There	そちら
昨日の夜(きのうよる) Last night	昨夜(さくや)	さっき Moments ago	先ほど(さき)	どっち Which	どちら
明日の朝(あしたあさ) Tomorrow morning	明朝(みょうちょう)	あとで Later	後ほど(のち)	ちょっと A little	少々(しょうしょう)
今日(きょう) Today	本日(ほんじつ)	前に(まえ) Before	以前(いぜん)	とても Very	大変(たいへん)
この間、この前(あいだ、まえ) The other day	先日(せんじつ)	すぐに Immediately	さっそく	すごく Extremely	非常に(ひじょう)
その日(ひ) That day	当日(とうじつ)	今回(こんかい) This time	このたび	どのくらい How much	いかほど
				〜くらい About 〜	〜ほど

● 相手(あいて)(客(きゃく))の〜、誰(だれ)かの〜 / Someone's (A customer's) 〜

主人(しゅじん) Husband	ご主人(様)(しゅじん)(さま)	おじいさん Grandfather	おじい様(さま)	娘(むすめ) Daughter	娘さん、(むすめ) お嬢様(じょうさま)
奥さん(おく) Wife	奥様(おくさま)	おばあさん Grandmother	おばあ様(さま)	家族(かぞく) Family	ご親族様(しんぞくさま)
父(ちち) Father	お父様(とうさま)	子供(こども) Child	お子様(方)(こさまがた)、お子さん	親戚(しんせき) Relatives	ご親戚様(しんせきさま)
母(はは) Mother	お母様(かあさま)	息子(むすこ) Son	息子さん(むすこ)、お坊ちゃま(ぼっ)	友人(ゆうじん) Friend	ご友人、(ゆうじん) お友達(ともだち)
両親(りょうしん) Parents	ご両親(様)(りょうしん)(さま)				

丁寧表現早見表

通常	丁寧	通常	丁寧	通常	丁寧
客、お客さん（きゃく、おきゃくさん）Customer	お客様（おきゃくさま）	会社（かいしゃ）Company	貴社、御社（きしゃ、おんしゃ）	家（いえ）Home	お宅、ご自宅（おたく、ごじたく）
皆さん（みなさん）Everybody	皆様（みなさま）	手紙（てがみ）Letter	お手紙、お便り（おてがみ、おたより）	返事（へんじ）Reply	お返事（おへんじ）
あの人（あのひと）That person	あちらの方（あちらのかた）	名前（なまえ）Name	お名前（おなまえ）	答え（こたえ）Answer	お答え、ご回答（おこたえ、ごかいとう）
この人（このひと）This person	こちらの方（こちらのかた）	住所（じゅうしょ）Address	ご住所（ごじゅうしょ）		

● 自分の～、自分の店の～ ／ My ~, Our store's ~

通常	丁寧	通常	丁寧	通常	丁寧
私（わたし）Me	私（わたくし）	店（みせ）Store	当店（とうてん）	係（かかり）Person in charge	係の者（かかりのもの）
私たち（わたしたち）Us	私ども（わたくしども）	会社（かいしゃ）Company	小社、当社、弊社（しょうしゃ、とうしゃ、へいしゃ）	担当者（たんとうしゃ）Person in charge	担当の者（たんとうのもの）
				店員（てんいん）Store employee	店の者（みせのもの）

4.「お〜」「ご〜」の表現 ／ O ~ and Go ~ Expressions

● お〜 ／ O ~

主に名詞・形容詞・動詞「Vます」に付く。／ Primarily attached to nouns, adjectives, and "(V) ~~masu~~."

お車（くるま）Car	お皿（さら）Plate	お料理（りょうり）Food	お部屋（へや）Room	お風邪（かぜ）Cold	お疲れ（つか）Tired
お体（からだ）Body	お食事（しょくじ）Meal	お荷物（にもつ）Luggage	お友達（ともだち）Friend	お祝い（いわい）Congratulations	お好き（な）（す）Favorite
お席（せき）Seat	お時間（じかん）Time	お品物（しなもの）Goods	お会計（かいけい）Bill	お急ぎ（いそ）Hurry	お忙しい（いそが）Busy
お肉（にく）Meat	お電話（でんわ）Telephone call	お名前（なまえ）Name	お仕事（しごと）Work	お済み（す）Completed	お得（な）（とく）Economical

● ご〜 ／ Go ~

主に名詞・動詞「Vする」に付く。／ Primarily attached to nouns and "V ~~suru~~."

ご本（ほん）Book	ご案内（あんない）Guidance	ご住所（じゅうしょ）Address	ご気分（きぶん）Mood	ご注意（ちゅうい）Warning	ご満足（まんぞく）Satisfaction
ご注文（ちゅうもん）Order	ご連絡（れんらく）Contact	ご署名（しょめい）Signature	ご出発（しゅっぱつ）Departure	ご相談（そうだん）Consultation	ご迷惑（めいわく）Bothersome
ご希望（きぼう）Desire	ご家族（かぞく）Family	ご伝言（でんごん）Message	ご招待（しょうたい）Invitation	ご協力（きょうりょく）Cooperation	ご無理（むり）Difficulty; impossibility
ご予約（よやく）Reservation	ご友人（ゆうじん）Friend	ご病気（びょうき）Sickness	ご説明（せつめい）Explanation	ご興味（きょうみ）Interest	

● 監修者・著者

水谷 信子（お茶の水女子大学・明海大学名誉教授、元アメリカ・カナダ大学連合日本研究センター教授、元ラジオ講座「100万人の英語」講師など）

● 著者

高橋尚子（熊本外語専門学校専任講師）、**スーザン・マスト**（元立命館大学英語講師、元オハイオ州立大学日本語講師）、**有田聡子**（弥勒の里国際文化学院日本語学校専任講師）、**寺田則子**（北京科技大学国際学院国際事業部長、大阪電気通信大学国際交流センター日本語教育担当）

カバーデザイン	花本浩一
本文デザイン／DTP	オッコの木スタジオ
カバー・本文イラスト	藤井アキヒト
翻訳	Alex Ko Ransom ／ Jenine Heaton ／ Ako Lindstrom
ナレーション	Bianca Allen ／都さゆり
協力	井上純子

すぐに使える 接客日本語会話大特訓 [英語版] 決まり文句700

平成28年（2016年）10月10日　初版第1刷発行
平成31年（2019年）　4月10日　　　　第2刷発行

監修者　水谷信子
著　者　水谷信子／高橋尚子／スーザン・マスト／有田聡子／寺田則子
発行人　福田富与
発行所　有限会社Jリサーチ出版
　　　　〒166-0002　東京都杉並区高円寺北2-29-14-705
電　話　03(6808)8801（代）　FAX 03(5364)5310
編集部　03(6808)8806
　　　　http://www.jresearch.co.jp
印刷所　中央精版印刷株式会社

ISBN 978-4-86392-312-6
禁無断転載。なお、乱丁、落丁はお取り替えいたします。

©2016 Nobuko Mizutani, Naoko Takahashi, Susan Mast, Satoko Arita, Noriko Terada All rights reserved.
Printed in Japan

How to Download Voice Data

STEP 1
Access the voice download website!

(Input the following URL:)
URL：http://febe.jp/jresearch

STEP 2
Continue to the FeBe registration page from the one displayed to register as a member.

Click 「FeBeに会員登録(無料)」
(Register to be a FeBe Member (Free))

※ To download voice data, you must register for the FeBe audiobook delivery service (registration is free).

Enter your email address, password (8 or more alphanumeric characters), name, birthday, and gender on the registration page ▶ Read the Terms of Service ▶ Click 「確認」(Confirm) ▶ Registration complete

STEP 3
Return to the download page from the 「ご登録が完了しました」page.

Click 「ダウンロードページ」(Download Page), then enter "23126" in the field under 「シリアルコードをご入力ください」(Please enter your serial code) on the page displayed and click 「送信」(Send).

STEP 4
Download voice data.

Click 「無料でオーディオブックを受け取る」 ▶ Click 「本棚で確認する」 ▶ Click 「ダウンロード」(Download 「全体版」)

※ If you are using a PC, please download voice data from 「本棚」. If you are using a smartphone, a guide will appear for the FeBe app. Please use the voice files through the app.

❗ Notice

- Voice data can be played from your PC, your iPhone, or your Android smartphone.
- Voice data can be downloaded and played as many times as you wish.
- For questions about downloads, please contact: info@febe.jp (Emails will be received from 10 AM to 8 PM on weekdays).